Arctic Ocean

BERING
SEA

Kamchatka

Sea of
Okhotsk

Sakhalin Island

Kuril Islands

Lena

A

LAKE
BAIKAL

Amur

Sea of
Japan

kutsk

• Ulan Ude

CHINA

Vladivostok

• Ulan Bator

JAPAN

• Tokyo

NGOLIA

KOREA DPR

Pyongyang

KOREA
REP. OF

• Seoul

Beijing •

Yellow Sea

AROUND THE SACRED SEA

With best wishes,

AROUND THE SACRED SEA

Mongolia and Lake Baikal on Horseback

BARTLE BULL

PHOTOGRAPHS BY

JOHN BOIT AND KERIM YALMAN

FIRST PUBLISHED IN THE UK IN 1999 BY
CANONGATE BOOKS LIMITED, 14 HIGH STREET, EDINBURGH EH1 1TE

COPYRIGHT © BARTLE BULL, 1999
THE MORAL RIGHTS OF THE AUTHOR HAVE BEEN ASSERTED.
PHOTOGRAPHS COPYRIGHT © JOHN BOIT AND KERIM YALMAN, 1999

THE LAKE BAIKAL WATERSHED PROJECT WAS SPONSORED BY THE EXPLORERS CLUB,
THE NATURAL RESOURCES DEFENSE COUNCIL, AND THE RUSSIAN ACADEMY OF SCIENCES.

DESIGNED AND TYPESET BY *et al*, LONDON

PRINTED IN HONG KONG

ISBN 0 86241 846 1

FOR MY MOTHER AND FATHER

CONTENTS

ACKNOWLEDGEMENTS

THIS UNDERTAKING has involved an expedition, an environmental project and a book – each of them new enough ground, for me, to have been inconceivable without the help I have received from friends and others.

John Adams at the Natural Resources Defense Council, Misha Gokhberg at the Russian Academy of Sciences, and John Bruno at the Explorers Club are the three men without whom our project could not have happened. Their personal support was as important as the sponsorship we received from their respective organisations.

At Harvard, Professors Jack Keenan and Nur Yalman introduced us to a world of khans and commissars while Professors Heinrich Holland and Ulrich Petersen revealed secrets of the limnologist, the logger and the volcano hunter. Professor John Edmonds at MIT helped us to develop our fieldwork program. Sir Ranulph Fiennes was a useful advisor during these preparatory days, as were Charles Swanson and my father, Bartle Bull.

Buck Knife, Cabella's, Kauffman Saddlery, Moss Tents, Patagonia, RayBan, Sierra Designs, Swiss Army Brands, and Willis & Geiger all provided us with very good equipment. William Hopkins and George Duffield organised a party, Dr Johannes Bartels gave us jabs, Bundy Boit made our sewing kits and Peter Toot designed our flag. Many individual backers contributed money and we are very grateful for their support and that of the Old Etonian Association.

With regard to the book, Julian Bach was encouraging and Robin Straus enthusiastic; Hope Davies introduced me to my publisher, Arabella Duffield, was tireless in research and other capacities, John Duffield gave me time off from work, Gavin Young taught me a valuable scrap or two of what he knows about writing, and my editors, Emily Dewhurst and Judy Moir, were much more forgiving and talented than I deserved.

Bartle Bull
November 1998

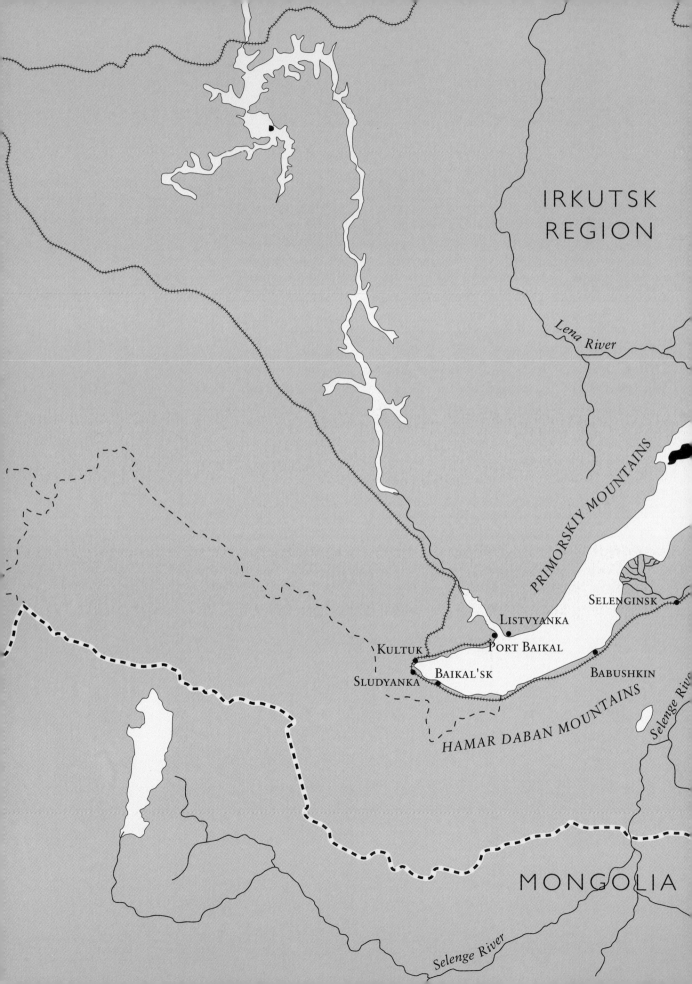

IRKUTSK
REGION

Lena River

PRIMORSKIY MOUNTAINS

SELENGINSK

Listvyanka

Kultuk   Port Baikal

Sludyanka   Baikal'sk

Babushkin

HAMAR DABAN MOUNTAINS

Selenge River

MONGOLIA

Selenge River

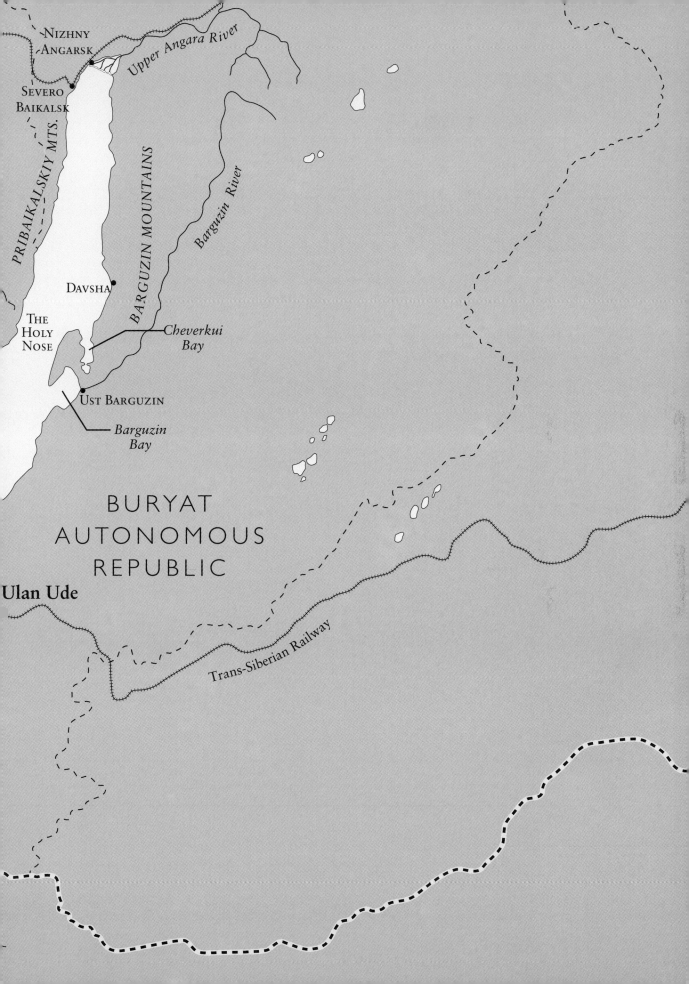

PROLOGUE

*A*T *the head of a party of eight men and ten horses, a stallion named Sarge and I are in the total blackness of a curved railway tunnel on the southwest shore of Siberia's Lake Baikal. It is the world's greatest lake and we are trying to ride all the way around it.*

Sarge almost died an hour ago, crashing through the spaces between the cross-ties of a decrepit railroad bridge. His strength and brute aggression saved him. Now I fear that I am the one about to suffer as I ride him, stumbling and bucking, through the tunnel's opacity. Unable to see even the reins I am holding, I can only sense Sarge's nostrils flaring and his ears straining ahead as he jigs sideways, forwards and back in his confusion.

I can feel his reins tighten and loosen in my left hand, but I cannot see the Mohawk-maned head that they lead to. In my right hand the lead rope of Malish, my pack-horse, alternately falls limp and wrenches backwards or out to either side. Without sight I have no sense of balance that the pressure of foot against stirrup does not provide. We grind against the jagged granite walls. We trip through tangled piles of wall-braces and wooden railroad ties, their rotting smell suiting the cool moisture of these mountain bowels.

Sarge staggers and darts to the left, jerking Malish's lead hard through my right hand. If I release the rope I lose Malish into the blackness. Almost suspended between the two horses, I pull back on Sarge's reins from an angle that brings him swinging round towards Malish, whose lead goes limp as Sarge and I lurch towards him. Suddenly I don't know where Malish is until a tent-pole strapped to his packsaddle jams into my thigh and his head and harness grind into my shoulder. In the commotion I have lost all bearings of forward and back. Sarge stumbles against a rock, his shoe ringing out in the gloom, two orange sparks illuminating nothing. Head to head now, facing in opposite directions in the tunnel, the two horses whinny and strain against each other, lead rope and reins entangled.

Quivering stallion energy, scared and aggressive, fills the dark in a mounting claustrophobic frenzy. Sarge neighs loudly in a frantic staccato that echoes around me. Somewhere in the blackness, hopefully behind us, the expedition's sole mare whinnies back. Sex is a palpable irritant to the brew of fear and stupid rage. Sarge starts to rear and buck.

Choking back my own panic, I swing out of the saddle and with my left hand follow Sarge's mane to his head. He is at least as scared as I am. I know this because I know him well, even when I cannot see him. I have spent the last month on his back. And he knows me: when I take his chin in the crook of my left arm he resists initially, but as I stroke the long bones of his nose I can feel his fear ebb with mine.

Opposite:
The Tamerlane
Expedition team
Left to right:
Nikolai Worp,
Kerim Yalman,
John Boit,
Bartle Bull and
Taran Davies
(J.B.)

I

This tunnel, like the other dozen through which we must pass before the week is out, is used by four trains a day at unpredictable hours. Behind us are five other men and eight more horses. If a train comes through now we will almost certainly lose horses. In the frenzy of animals crashing about we might well lose a man as well. A shot of morphine is the best medical care we can hope for. I work as quickly as possible to untangle the reins and rope and then I lead the horses on by foot. Sarge surges forward repeatedly. Each time my grip on his reins pulls him around until he collides with Malish or me. The tangles recur but we move forward, guided by the gravel mound on which the train-tracks are laid. After fifty yards a tiny white spot of light appears far ahead. I stop the horses and strain my ears for the sound of a train. Behind me the noises of my companions are low and rounded as if under water. Ahead the light is silent and still. It is the end of the tunnel. As we round the curve the pin-prick becomes a sliver and then bulges like a waxing moon. Soon the train-tracks carry parallel reflections of silver towards me through the blackness.

I emerge from the tomblike damp into the dry blue air of a Siberian summer, the kind of summer that is hot in windless sunlight but in which no breeze is a warm one. Towering up to my left are the lower cliffs of the Pribaikalskiy Mountains. To my right, fifty feet below and running north and south to the horizon, is Lake Baikal. It is the oldest, coldest, largest, cleanest and deepest of the world's lakes. It contains as much water as all five of America's Great Lakes combined. In its crystalline waters live fresh-water seals, 10-foot indigenous sturgeon, translucent golomyanka and fifteen hundred other species found nowhere else on the planet. Born twenty-five million years ago when the heavens themselves looked different, Baikal is twenty-four times older than walking man and twelve times as old as the next oldest lake, Lake Tanganyika. Protected against the filling effects of river-borne sediment by an annual seismic widening of 2.5 centimetres, Lake Baikal now holds about 70 per cent of all clear and uncontaminated fresh water known to man.

This reservoir, living museum of evolution, and pristine laboratory for the study of life is now threatened by pollution from towns, factories, logging, agriculture, ranching and acid rain. Five hundred tons of nitrates enter the lake from these sources annually. In the water around the effluent pipes of the Baikalsk pulp mill, several species have been found to be breeding in mutated form. The omul, a salmonid fish unique to Lake Baikal, a species long prized for its taste and nutritional value, rarely spawns naturally. Fish catches are declining; new congenital health disorders are appearing among the Buryat people of the lake's East Coast; migratory-bird counts are dwindling.

Despite the lake's isolated location deep in the cold heart of Siberia, the environmental depredations of the last generation are only the most recent chapter in the long and rich story of man's relationship with Lake Baikal. Genghis Khan was born near Baikal's southern shores sometime around 1167. In the nineteenth century the exiled Decembrists (members of the Russian conspiracy of December 1825) founded schools and libraries and string quartets for the communities of miners, fishermen, fur-trappers, traders and Cossacks who lived on the lake's shores and in the steppe and forest beyond. When the Trans-Siberian railway was built at the beginning of the twentieth century, a short stretch at Baikal's southern corner delayed completion for four years and claimed more workers' lives than the other five thousand miles of track combined. In 1916, to protect the finest of all species of sable, the original lifeblood of the Csarist treasury, Russia's first nature reserve was established on Baikal's north-east shore. At the end of the 1950s the Russian environmental movement was also born here, a response to Krushchev's insistence that 'Baikal must work.' To Russians from St Petersburg to Vladivostok, Lake Baikal is the physical touchstone of their country's soul. To the Buryats whose ancestors came here from the Mongol steppe two centuries before the birth of the Great Khan, Baikal is holy. It is the Sacred Sea.

I am a twenty-three-year-old New Yorker. How did I come to be here, with five other men and ten horses, high above Baikal's blue depths and far below the peaks that hold them in, with one long tunnel behind me and twelve more ahead?

Twenty months ago, on a rainy night in the garden of a Harvard club in Cambridge, Massachusetts, I told two good friends of a dream I had to ride horses across the greatest land-mass in the world. We sealed a pact with blood to do our damnedest to ride from Mongolia all the way to the Caspian Sea. We would follow the routes of Attila, Genghis and the Silk Route traders. Sharing an interest in environmental matters, we put together a programme of ecological work to help us raise money and to add backbone to our journey. After a year of planning darkened by mounting security worries, a man from the CIA told us that the steppe and mountains of Central Asia had become too lawless to risk the journey. 'If you go there', he said, 'you will die'.

So, with the help of our sponsors from the Explorers Club, the Russian Academy of Sciences and the Natural Resources Defense Council, we changed our plans. Motivated largely by the adventure but also by the work we would be doing on their behalf – collecting water samples, interviewing scientists, politicians, grass-roots activists, loggers, fishermen and so on, and generally gauging the scene from the perspective of educated laymen – we would follow the watershed of the Selenge River from Mongolia into the Autonomous Republic of Buryatia and north to Lake Baikal, of which we would then attempt the first continuous circumnavigation in history.

chapter one

ULAN BATOR

WHAT were we to expect as we approached Mongolia? For decades it had been the world's most closed and mysterious country. Now it was hard to imagine much beyond the old stereotypes. Would we find in this newly free land the hospitality and clear-eyed dignity typical among the world's herding peoples? Would we find that the scions of history's greatest warriors were bleak and degenerate, the spirit of the Scythians, the Huns and Genghis Khan's hordes addled by alcohol and seventy years of Communism, turned sullen in the post-Soviet depression?

These were my thoughts twenty thousand feet above the Gobi Desert on a May morning in 1993. The Russian-built Tupolev TU-154 of MIAT Mongolia Flight 224, en route from Beijing to Ulan Bator, was humming through a blue spring sky of adamantine brilliance. Below us the Gobi stretched bleakly to the horizon. My two companions and I had left university a few days previously and we would soon find ourselves on horseback far out on the Mongol steppe, riding north to Siberia.

History suggested that we would have to go carefully. In 1220, while his soldiers slaughtered thirty thousand citizens in the streets of Bokhara, Genghis Khan had ridden into the Great Mosque, ordered it converted to a stable, mounted the pulpit and proclaimed himself to be the 'Scourge of God'. To medieval Europeans, the Mongol hordes were just that – scourges of the Christian god.

In 1241, Pope Innocent IV wrote 'When we consider that through these Tartars the name of Christian might utterly perish, our bones shudder at the thought.'[1] Count Henry of Lorraine voiced the common sentiment that the Tartar invaders exploding out of the unknown steppe represented the Apocalypse itself: 'The dangers foretold in Scripture long ago are now springing up and erupting.'[2]

The Mongol threat elicited the extremes of Europe's Christian culture. The clergy led hysterical congregations in churches that were packed every day of the week throughout northern Europe. Trains of flagellants howled across the continent. In Germany Jews were slaughtered.

The Hungarians described the Mongol soldiery as 'dog-faced Tartars', and meant it literally. In 1238, as Europe cowered before the Mongol armies about to rampage through Hungary, Poland, Austria, the Balkans and northern Italy, Friar Jordan of Giano, a Franciscan vicar, articulated other fantasies of terror into which Western Christendom had fallen at the 'Tartar' advance:

Tamerlane, the great Tartar conqueror (1336 - 1405)

During the planning of our original route to the Caspian Sea our sponsors at the Russian Academy of Sciences suggested we name the expedition after him

5

The Mongol woman who fights best is regarded as the most desirable, just as in our society she who weaves and sews best is regarded as more desired than the one who is beautiful. They eat frogs, dogs, serpents, and all things alike. The men are inhuman and of the nature of beasts rather to be called monsters than men, thirsting after and drinking blood, and tearing and devouring the flesh of dogs and human beings... [3]

If this was what we were to expect we were in for a hell of a ride.

After a couple of hours the Gobi began to give way to the southerly reaches of the central Mongolian steppe, where an unusually long winter was just ending. The snows had largely melted but the steppe was not yet green and all we could see were arid brown ridges and gentle valleys wrinkled along the paths of thirsty rivers.

From the air it all seemed tougher, emptier, more haunting than we had imagined. Mongolia is a country larger than the United Kingdom, Ireland, France, Italy and Germany combined, inhabited by a population that is less than a third of London's. Chills ran up my spine as the landing gear locked down. It had been nearly two years since I had first broached the idea of this expedition on that wet night in the garden at Harvard.

With me on the plane were two of my best friends: Nikolai Worp and John Boit. Nikolai was an Amsterdam boulevardier whose claims to have been a member of the Dutch national ski team we overlooked in favour of the volunteer work he'd done with the Emergency Medical Service while studying at New York's Columbia University. John, a Maine Yankee, was to be one of the expedition's two photographers. The other was to be Kerim Yalman, a Russian-speaking Turk who would join us at the Siberian border in a few weeks. Yalman and Taran Davies, an Englishman who was hoping to make a television documentary about the expedition, were still at Harvard, handling last-minute fund raising and scrambling to complete the logistical preparations with our sponsors at the Russian Academy of Sciences.

At the Trade Union Hotel, Nikolai, John and I had our first whiff of the boiled mutton-fat odour that seems to pervade every Mongol structure. The smell, a mix of caramel and old socks, was so different from that of lamb chops that I wondered how the two could come from the same animal. We ditched our bags in our bedroom and headed out on foot to meet Sean Hinton, an English ethnomusicologist whom we had engaged to set up our Mongolian logistics. We took with us one of the saddles we had brought from home, so that Hinton could show it to our Mongol guide. Hinton, an important man from our point of view, gave us an immediate feeling of confidence. He didn't hesitate to make it clear that we would never be able to fool him into thinking we knew what we were doing. It would not have taken a member of Mensa to read us as he did, but we soon saw from his wit and his insights about Mongolia that he was intelligent as well as honest.

Darkness had fallen by the time we headed out of his flat in search of a drink. It was a cold, clear night, a few degrees below freezing. Even in the middle of the city we could see our first Inner Asian stars, bright little *amuses bouches* presaging the four-month feast that lay ahead. Our primary concern, however, was distinctly terrestrial: to get to the Ulan Bator Hotel or anywhere else we could find a cold beer. We had read and heard that Mongol toughs had taken to beating up the few Russian soldiers still stationed in the capital after the official 'last Russian soldier' had left eight months previously. Nik, John and I, with our short blond hair, bush trousers and big trekking boots that fairly shouted 'Russki conscript', stayed alert as we passed down the dimly lit streets. At a busy intersection a crowd of young Mongols was milling about, and we took a few jostles and glares as we walked through the *mêlée*. A youth of about our age walked up to me, made a pistol shape with his right fist, stuck his forefinger to my temple, and shouted 'Bam!' with a grotesque smile. We walked on.

At the Ulan Bator Hotel, we found the entrance to the bar blocked by a pair of sturdy Mongol bouncers. The predictable mess of tarts, drunk expats and awkwardly slick young locals milled about the corridor. After a brief wait we were ushered inside. The marginal but self-important chaos inside was not the only thing that made me think of the United Nations. Immortalised in Nick Middleton's *Last Disco in Outer Mongolia*, the place had a most international feel. The beers were Singaporean, the pop music French, the whores Mongolian, and the drunks Russian. The universal language of lust emanated loudly from several dark tables.

Seven and a half centuries earlier, in its imperial heyday, the Mongol capital at Karakorum had been even more cosmopolitan. In 1246, two Franciscan monks, emissaries of Pope Innocent IV, attended the investiture of Genghis' grandson Kuyuk as the third Great Khan. Friar John of Plano Carpini and Friar Benedict the Pole were among no less than four thousand ambassadors from the tribes and nations that the Mongols had conquered or impressed with the need for representation at the great ceremony. According to Friar John's report, the high bureaucrats of the Mongol empire included Chinese and Muslims; the new Khan's mother, a Nestorian Christian, was in thrall to a Persian slave girl called Fatima; and the imperial throne and seal had been made by a Russian goldsmith. Some of the many Nestorian Christians serving as clerks at Kuyuk's court had encouraged the friars with reports that Kuyuk favoured their religion above the many others also tolerated in his domain.

Another Franciscan friar, a Fleming known as William of Rubruck, visited Karakorum itself in 1254. There he found twelve Buddhist, Taoist and Shamanist temples, two mosques, and one Nestorian church. The imperial palace, then occupied by Mongke, who had succeeded his cousin Kuyuk as supreme khan when the latter had drunk himself to death after two years on the throne, was Chinese in style. Within was a silver drinking fountain designed by a Parisian goldsmith called Buchier, one of many European craftsmen at the court. From this fountain flowed wine and the fermented milk of the imperial mares.

The revelries taking place before our eyes at the Last Disco in Outer Mongolia had more in common with the courts of the great khans than just an international atmosphere. Even at the pinnacle of the Mongols' conquering vigour, drinking was a major feature of their life. Several of Genghis' successors drank themselves to death and one of them, his son and heir Ogedei, did so despite promising to halve the number of cups of wine he imbibed daily. Genghis had built his empire, the largest the world had yet seen, as much on cunning as on fortitude and brutality and Ogedei proved himself a worthy successor by commissioning a double-sized goblet so that he could honour his promise.

We spent the next two days undertaking a variety of chores in Ulan Bator. On a street where Ulan Bator's drunks congregate in an atmosphere of mild violence and extreme stupefaction, we bought a pound of cayenne pepper, hoping it would be enough to overwhelm whatever mutton the steppe sent our way. We went to the US Embassy to register ourselves, but the door was locked, the lights were out and the only Marine on duty was artfully disguised as a hunch-backed Mongolian gardener who spoke no English. Later we cruised the shops looking for something with which to mute the bright blue of our saddle bags, which we feared might attract attention on the steppe. Dark paint would have done the trick, but we were told at every stop that there was no paint to be found in Ulan Bator that spring. Finally we found some black Chinese hair-dye and headed back to the Trade Union Hotel. By the time I had finished dyeing the bags our room looked like the site of a convention of six-year-old Dadaists.

At times, as we walked the streets on our various chores, we found something not quite beautiful but certainly rather fetching about Ulan Bator. The wife of the last mayor was said to have been a great lover of children, and in every square and courtyard we saw surprising numbers of them playing on swings or climbing-frames. Soviet-era follies and neon signs lent a pleasing absurdity to the rows of dignified monoliths ornamented with sober pilasters and geometric iron-work. At other times the crumbling half-built buildings and abandoned piles of bricks made the city look like the newspaper photographs of Sarajevo, or perhaps an architectural dig – a stunning find from the Stalinist epoch. Inside, every building smelled strongly of mutton. The decaying public corridors were tidy and clean. Whether they wore bright Chinese acrylics or the traditional robe-like braided *del*, the people we saw on the streets were uncommonly fastidious with their appearance, showing a degree of outward pride or vanity that is not nearly so widespread in New York and London.

We ate our final urban dinner in a restaurant that was said to be Ulan Bator's last vestige of the Soviet raj: it was run by a Russian, served Russian caviar and beef and wines, and accepted only the loftiest Mongol patrons. Hinton warned us at dinner that booze was the greatest danger we faced on the trail that lay ahead of us. Our guides had sworn in writing not to drink during the expedition. 'If you want a drink', warned Hinton, 'drink it discreetly'.

That afternoon, at Hinton's flat, we had met our guide to discuss food, the route and our equipment. We were impressed by Bazra, a part-time hunter and a man of the steppe. He was a wiry fellow with sharp features which gave him a look of intelligence. His manner was reserved and beneath it lay a twinkle that emerged when he spoke of the journey ahead. He said the route north to our Siberian rendezvous would take us through some of his country's most beautiful terrain, both through classic Mongol steppeland and over the Hentei Mountains of the Siberian frontier lands. No outsider, he said, had ever reached the Russian border by this route.

1 Marshall, R. (1993) *Storm from the East: From Genghis Khan to Kubilai Khan, London.*
2 Ibid.
3 Ibid.

chapter two

THE STEPPE

AFTER our third Ulan Bator breakfast of mutton and sugared rice we piled our packs and saddles into an old Red Army equivalent of a Bedford lorry and headed out to the steppe. The drive took us south and west deep into the spare, rolling prairies of the ancient Mongol heartlands.

Opposite:
Riding across
the steppe
(J.B.)

The Selenge River, Lake Baikal's principal tributary, begins its thousand-mile journey north in the foothills of the Khangai Mountains of western-central Mongolia. Numerous other streams join it along the way and our journey was to begin in this great bowl of pastureland providing the sources of the river that ultimately contributes half of Lake Baikal's water. In these deepest reaches of Baikal's watershed we expected to find little human activity other than nomads tending their herds of sheep, yaks and horses.

Our base camp lay in the flat of a broad valley with a wide, shallow stream running through it and brown hills crumpling away in every direction. That first day was bright and with the wind blowing hard from shifting directions we found ourselves squinting throughout the morning as we met our Mongol companions, repacked and sorted the bags of food, tents and clothing, and discussed final details with Hinton. We didn't stop squinting until we reached the forested foothills of the Hentei Mountains two weeks later. Even in the short season between the snows the steppe weather is harsh and unpredictable, searing the eyes of its people into a slit so constant that in most of our photographs from the steppe it was difficult to discern whether the eyes of the Mongols were open or closed.

With Bazra at the camp were the three other Mongols who were to ride with us. Nyamba, an Assistant Professor of Soil Science at the Mongolian State University, was rounder and less weathered than Bazra. Understanding and sympathising with our objectives, he would be useful as we made decisions en route. Enke, the only woman in our party, was a thirty-year-old schoolteacher with a face as round and cheery as a child's smiley-face drawing. She was to be translator and, we were delighted to hear, cook.

Enke's lively spirit and patent enthusiasm for the journey ahead made a deep contrast to the ghastly decrepitude of Dorj, our fourth Mongol companion. He was the brother of the man from whom Bazra had rented our horses and he had been sent along to see that they all got back to their summer pastures. Dorj was decaying by the hour. He shambled about the camp with stooped shoulders and the sunken cheeks, gap-teeth and bleary eyes of a Dodge City degenerate who'd seen too many long poker games go the wrong way. We called him the Gambler.

'Bazra', I asked, 'is this man really ready for a hard ride?'

'Bull', said Bazra, 'he only forty years old. He Mongol man. No problem.'

We first saw our thirteen horses when they came trotting over a small rise to the north of the camp, led by a Mongol on horseback. Surrounded by the steppe, that wondrous, mythical place of my boyhood imagination, we had been waiting, our bags and saddles in a pile at our feet. After two years of planning, four months of prairie, mountain and forest lay ahead. These horses would start us on our way and the thrumming of their hooves approaching over the prairie found an echo in my quickened heartbeat.

Opposite:
A Mongol saddle
(J.B.)

The rider was Dorj's brother, the owner of the horses. The silver ornaments of his saddle and bridle flashed at us across the steppe as he rode. When he dismounted and walked towards us with a mariner's rolling gait it was obvious that he was a Mongol of the kind that disdains any life not lived in the saddle. Clearly a man of substance – none other could have spared so many horses – he met us with brusque, dismissive dignity suitable to his station and his superior existence. Embodying all of this was his ancestral wooden saddle, its high front and back forming a U, painted ochre, decorated with silver medallions and frayed red velvet, its tooled leather thigh wings painted in geometrical patterns of crimson and yellow. For a hat he wore a traditional Mongol skull-cap, spiked at the top, made of crimson silk and edged in gold braid. On his body he wore a grey del, the long, high-collared double-breasted gown, fastened about the waist with a silk sash, that is the Mongol's national dress. His traditional calf-length boots, ostentatiously ill-suited to travelling by foot, were made of embroidered felt and their sharp toes curled upwards.

When he had taken a cup of fat-sweetened tea by the fire, he introduced us to his horses. Having just emerged from a long winter on the steppe, they were so thin that their rear hip-bones stuck out like the tail-fins of old Cadillacs. There was not one of them on which we couldn't count the ribs. Their heads looked too big for their bodies and their manes and tails were so long that anywhere else they would have looked frivolous.

Bazra had inspected our saddles two days previously in Hinton's flat. He had approved, but we were nonetheless pleased to confirm at first hand that they were a good fit. The saddles – compact, lightweight versions of the traditional pommelled American cowboy design – attracted admiring grunts and inquisitive touches from every Mongol present. Even the Gambler was moved to a show of enthusiasm. The saddle bags, each pair carrying rain gear, canteens, a hatchet, a bowl, a mug, a spoon, and waterproof matches, had benefited from being dyed black at the Trade Union Hotel. In the days of the Great Khan, the Mongol hordes

rode with saddle bags made from the stomachs of yaks, which would be inflated and used as floats for major river crossings.

Before we rode off, Enke cooked a sweet mutton stew. As we ate, the prized fatty bits floating salty and elusive around our bowls, Bazra and Nyamba seemed restless, eager to hit the trail. When they discussed the emptiness of the steppe, a longing, like the glow of a coal when the ash is blown off, lit their eyes.

In Mongolia, rain at the start of a journey is auspicious. As we rode off from the base camp it drizzled coyly but did not rain. After about fifteen miles we made camp a few hundred yards beyond a tableau of old Buddhist rock drawings barely discernible on the stone face of a low cliff. On drawing our attention to these, Nyamba had also pointed out a spot farther down the cliff where he claimed Russian artillerymen had used similar drawings for target practice in the 1970s. Bazra spat bitterly into the ground as Nyamba explained the story.

Sheltered under a stand of poplars gathered in the crook of a small, rocky stream, with four valleys stretching away in their various directions, our first campsite was as pretty as we had ever hoped it would be. The clear stream, cooled by the melting mountain snows, murmured calmly past us as we washed our hands in preparation for the first of hundreds of meals by a fire. Our right hands were raw and stiff from dragging the pack-horses and the icy water was a relief. In the animistic world view of the ancient and medieval Mongols running water was alive and the *yasa*, the old body of law governing life on the steppe that began to take formal shape under Genghis, had forbidden washing or urinating in streams and rivers.

Before supper the camp settled down to a brief hour of quiet. I started to read *The Brothers Karamazov*. My father had given it to me, a wonderfully appropriate present, not so much because it was about parricides as because, being a Russian novel, it was culturally germane and thick enough to double as a pillow.

Later that evening Enke cooked a rack of sheep ribs over the fire. Compared with the customary Mongol practice of boiling mutton in a stew, Enke's barbecue was an extravagance.

'Boys very lucky,' said Bazra, looking at the fat dripping into the coals. Each pop meant the loss of a few more calories, each long sizzle a hundred yards of strength. When mutton is stewed none of the fat is wasted, and the greasy residue protects one's lips from the bitter climate of the open plains. The bright evening light belied the cool air and we stayed near the coals as Nyamba gave us a surprisingly technical lesson in stripping the bones clean. Afterwards he gave us a big handful of wild garlic from the river bank. After supper we sat by the fire. We drank tea,

Opposite:
Two Mongolian women of high birth, *circa* 1910

smoked and talked. In surprisingly sentimental tones Bazra and Nyamba showed a deep interest in the American Indian, with whom Mongols share nomadism, shamanism, and various long-obscured fragments of ethnic heritage. 'Mongol man have brothers everywhere. Baikal, America, South America, Turkey, Eskimo, everywhere,' said Bazra.

As we rode through Mongolia we were often surprised at the depth and emotional intensity of many Mongols' preoccupation with their cultural identity. In matters of nature, language, history and ethnicity we saw it again and again. That first night, Nyamba went so far as to say that Mongol and American Indian babies were both known occasionally to be born with blue dots on their bottoms. It seemed bizarre, but I discovered long after the expedition that Nyamba had been correct.

As the spring chill deepened around the fire and the lowering darkness revealed diamond patches of stars among the clouds, Bazra sang a lilting Mongol lyric about the Yoroo River. It was a couple of hundred miles to our north; soon enough we would see it for ourselves.

MORNING OF 2ND JUNE, THE STEPPE SOUTH-WEST OF ULAN BATOR

I awoke this morning to a cheery 'Happy Birthday, Bull!' from Nik. John, true to his undergraduate form, was the last to rise and also bade me a happy birthday. I am twenty-three.

It is a cloudless morning, warming up rapidly, and the day promises to be harsh and dry. But out here, who knows. All of us, the Mongols not least, are hungry for whatever today's trail will bring. After days of the broad plains we are approaching a stretch of hilly, forested country ill-suited to herding. The steppe has been wild and empty but we're hungry for the forested wilderness that awaits us.

LUNCH, THE SAME DAY

It's been a quiet and eerie half a day. We've been winding northwards along a marshy valley, pulling the packhorses through a drab, desolate landscape in which nothing moves except the clouds, every colour is dreary in the flat overcast light, and no sounds are to be heard other than the rustle and clatter of our horses' unshod hooves on grass and rock. A tugging wind has blown all day, as it has every day, and our eyes are squinty and our lips already cracked. The hills on either side are covered with silvery pines and the valley floor has the purple-grey tone of heather. The footing is rock-strewn and boggy. The going is slow but easy compared with what we expect in the forested passes of the Hentei Mountains farther north. At least in the woods we shall escape the wind.

For now the landscape is a wind-bitten cross between Scottish moorland and the Montana Big Sky. We see no more lonely cattle and sheep, no more domestic animals of any sort, no people. We have spotted one moose and often we hear cuckoo birds. The wind is gusting up and its low whistle carries the fatty smell of our roasting mutton. In half an hour we shall be back in the saddle, pushing north. Overhead, the stern naval clouds sail towards the eastern horizon, oblivious to these small thoughts of small men on the vast steppe.

3RD JUNE, THE STEPPE

During a short rest before supper last night, John and I were saying that we couldn't be much happier. We were sitting with a mug of whisky on a fifteen-foot embankment over the Bayangol River, our first stretch of what will ultimately become Baikal water.

The Bayangol was mostly a thick layer of white ice snaking flat and bright through a rocky wilderness of brown and green. The day had provided a long and pretty ride that had taken us as far as we had planned. The fire was sparking and popping away and supper was on it. Life couldn't get much better. And then Nik came up with a small package, a birthday present from my father. It contained eight long Havana cigars, a note and a photograph of our house in the valley of the Hudson River. Mutton shanks around the fire made a delicious dinner on the river bank. Afterwards, John, Nik and I smoked the cigars, drank whisky, and read out loud those two Robert Service poems so beloved of wandering spirits, 'The Shooting of Dan McGrew' and 'The Cremation of Sam McGee'.

Today's ride was a long one but we got where we wanted to go. It was our first day in tough terrain, and there is a feeling of mild exhilaration at having reached our destination. Our camp and pasture are on an island in the middle of a stream watering the floor of yet another broad valley. The land around us is mostly open pastureland with a few cultivated fields, the first that we have seen in Mongolia.

To get here we descended out of the mountains through the thick wilderness of the alpine uplands. We rode through tangled groves of poplar, birch, and larch and along steep, stream-cut slopes. As the horses picked their way through the deadfall and over the rocks, the dark mountainsides were quiet and calm as the moon. Even the birds were silent.

Early this evening, shortly after we had emerged from this steep, untracked bush into a more familiar landscape of rolling prairie, we passed through the first settlement we have seen since Ulan Bator. It was a decrepit village of about twenty wooden houses laid out along a single street. The street was empty and quiet save for the low whimpering of a balding custard-coloured mongrel trailing us from doorway to doorway. Apparently taking us for Russians, bitter from seventy years under the Soviet yoke, mothers and children watched silently from doorways, staring at us with weary hatred. At first we had tried smiling or waving at the villagers, but the dogged resentment in their eyes soon stopped us.

Nyamba is going home tomorrow. Bazra says this is because his wife is ill. Nyamba cites Examination period at the University, saying that the President gave him only four days off. On Nikolai's prompting we have gently indicated to Bazra that while we don't appreciate the excuses we accept Nyamba's departure. Bazra will replace him with a man called Nyamdorj, a hunting companion from a settlement nearby.

The Gambler, meanwhile, is hanging on, struggling to contribute and managing a brave grin a few times a day. Had he any vigour whatsoever he would resemble Death himself.

7:10 P.M., 4TH JUNE, THE WEST BANK OF THE HARAA RIVER

After supper last night we sat around the fire with our new companion and two other friends of Bazra's. The former, a weatherbeaten, stocky man of about forty, is called Nyamdorj. He seems solid enough but only time and the trail will tell. The other two arrived an hour after Nyamdorj and from a different direction. They were hunters from the Tuva tribe, the Reindeer People of the Lake Hoopsugul region where north-eastern Mongolia bulges up beyond the steppe and into Siberia's forested underbelly.

I remembered Hinton telling us that once the Mongols started drinking they would consume all drink within reach, even if it took a few days to do so. He'd gone so far as to make Bazra swear in writing that he wouldn't drink during the journey. He'd also asked Bazra to swear that he wouldn't bring any vodka with him on the expedition, but Bazra had objected, saying that the horses were weak after the winter and might need a drink from time to time.

Opposite:
A *ger*
(J.B.)

So it was tense around the fire as Bazra showed us the bottle and opened it. Bazra was breaking his oath and he knew we knew it. The village we had ridden through that afternoon had reminded us how exposed we were and how tough an environment the steppe is. The last thing we needed was a three-day binge of firewater and brawling. But in front of the visitors Bazra's pride was at stake and we decided to accept a ceremonial libation and try to keep things steady from there. And anyway, we felt like a drink and a talk with these hunters and reindeer herders under the Inner Asian stars.

Bazra passed me Nyamba's traditional wooden bowl, shallow and inlaid with silver, for the first drink. I had forgotten to watch Bazra pour out the measure but when I saw Nik smirk I knew I was in trouble. The smell nearly etherised me as I took the bowl in both hands. I felt like a child being force-fed that last cold spoonful of peas. It took all of my undergraduate training to maintain a smile and a scrap of dignity as I passed the bowl to the Tuva hunter on my right. The bowl went around three times and soon Bazra was putting his arm around anybody in reach and saying in English 'Mongolia beautiful country, beautiful country.'

We had another long talk around the fire. Bazra and Nyamba know the history of their people and speak with knowledge and love about their country and its regions. They care deeply about preserving the natural and cultural character of Mongolia and seem to understand that development and population growth are not always the path to happiness. They loathe the Communists and know well the indignities that Mongolia suffered at the hands of the Slav during the past seventy years. They speak wistfully of the Buryats, the Kalmuks and the Oirats, their brother Mongols fenced into Russia by modern borders.

Two more bottles were soon cajoled out of the visitors and when there was none left they drifted off into the dark. When we retired to our tent Bazra was alone by the fire, singing sloppily in a muted, squeaky voice while Nyamba snored nearby. Enke had retired long before.

This morning we cut across several high downs, rejoining the Haraa River at lunch time. After the meal and into the evening we followed the Haraa north. Still half-brown after the winter, the steppe is harsh in texture and colour but more lush every day. Valley after valley, rise after depression after rise, the plains rolled on as we rode.

Three times we saw little white dots against the green and brown expanse, like sun-bleached sand-dollars on a duney beach. As we neared the dots they took shape as isolated gers (the round, felt tents often called yurts in English). They all looked trim with their brave little lines of pine trees and their small vegetable plots pitted against the dry, rocky soil. At each encampment, horses stood tethered and ready under saddles bedecked with silver, frayed silk and tooled leather. At two of the gers, log cabins were being built, their eaves decorated with simple geometrical carvings.

It is desolate country and we wondered where the herdsmen who live in those gers find wood for cooking and building. Their winter pastures are in valleys bordered by forests providing wind-breaks and firewood for the cold months. Now, in the spring pastures, smoke rose from holes in the centre of each ger's roof but there were usually no trees for hundreds of yards, and very few at that. When John asked, Bazra said that the nomads burn dung when they have no wood.

Opposite:
Above:
Carcasses after the Winter
(J.B.)

Below:
Bazra
(J.B.)

The day we rode through was wet and blustery, the temperature just above freezing. For almost seven months a year, between October and May, the Mongols and their herds weather temperatures that often descend to fifty below zero. We have passed dozens of the freshly rot-ting carcases of domestic animals culled by the latest winter.

Night falls at about ten o'clock and on sunny days we can usually ride until eight or a little later. Today, we stopped earlier because a remote prison village is on the path ahead and we wanted to spend the night well clear of it. We hope to reach our next main destination, a semi-permanent encampment of gers where provisions are said to await, during the afternoon of the day after tomorrow.

The Trans-Siberian railroad in these parts is a ramshackle affair occasionally accompanied by rotting, listing telephone poles and collapsing sheds. There is no other mark of man in any direc-tion and to the train traveller it must look a cruel and mysterious landscape. From the saddle it is different. The landscape is very much alive, even human. Travelling by horseback and living on the ground, the terrain and its vastness are tougher and bigger than they are to the mechanised traveller, but they become tangible, readable, accessible to our understanding. Our eyes and thoughts adapt, learning that each large valley, opening out into apparently endless webs of others of its kind, is not so intimidating and endless as it seems. An hour later, we are always at the crest of a new hill, or at an unexpected bend in the river, and the way is filled with small, engrossing sights and dramas: black and white pika-pika birds, wrenching tugs from pack-horses, the 'kuk... kooo' of the cuckoo birds that we look for but never see, rainbows of wildflowers, white bones of horses and sheep.

We did some singing on the trail today and soon discovered that the horses prefer the stirring 'Rolling, rolling, rolling...' chords of 'Rawhide'. Whenever we sing it our animals line up three abreast and carry us forward at a surging trot. Clearly a tune to be saved for emergencies.

7:55 P.M., 5TH JUNE, THE WEST BANK OF THE HARAA RIVER

The fire is crackling and dinner is cooking. We are weary but the camp is in a pretty place. It's a typical pre-dinner scene. Enke is cooking, Bazra and the Gambler are seeing to the horses, and Nyamdorj is collecting firewood. John is fishing for the pot, Nik is reading his medical field manuals and I am scribbling. We have washed our hands and faces and are refreshed and ready for our next mutton soup. We are hungry and soon will eat. When things are like this at the end of a long day it usually feels pretty good.

But today we haven't moved an inch towards our destination. Two of our horses disappeared early this morning, between six o'clock and saddling-up. They were unhobbled and as they grazed they must have drifted off over the long, low ridge sloping down to the short flat of valley floor in which we are camped. We have spent the day riding out in various directions on this side of the Haraa, talking to the three families of local herdsmen and looking fruitlessly for

the horses. We should have found them relatively easily, considering that horses don't stray permanently from their packs without being chased or led.

On various occasions in the last few days we have seen herdless riders, one or two at a time, watching us from ridges and hill-tops in the middle distance. We have twice suggested to Bazra that a night watch might be a good idea but each time he shrugged us off. Rustling, like herding and living in felt gers, remains a part of steppe life and we, as obvious strangers to these parts, must offer a tempting target. Once our horses had wandered over the ridge and out of view of the camp, they would have been easy prey. And, as Bazra explained, a good rustler has no shortage of ways to coax a horse over a hill.

None of the nomads around here admit to having enough horses to consider selling one or two to us, although we suspect that they have their own reasons for wanting to limit our mobility. Meanwhile Bazra, the Gambler and Nyamdorj are not known in the environs, so nobody will trust us to rent or borrow mounts.

The horses we have are still thin, although despite the hundred or so miles we have covered they appear to be recovering from their winter's ordeal. The load from the two stolen horses will be shared out among those that remain and we should be able to continue our progress north to Russia. We shall leave the nomads' pastureland for the forest wilderness after our next re-supply point, a day's ride from here.

Rain fell in the nearby mountains this morning and now the river is rising and muddy. We are grateful for this excuse for our failures with rod and reel.

AFTER SUPPER

It is 9:30 now and still light, although cloudy. The ragged wind persists. The air has a penetrating, damp chill and we will sleep, as we ate, to the sounds of the river and the shuffling, munching horses. Nik is reading Medicine for Mountaineering *and John is whittling. He is not certain what he is making. The log that Enke was sitting on has collapsed and she lies giggling on the ground. Bazra is making duck calls by sucking on a piece of plastic bag. Owls respond. Perhaps he should hoot.*

The next day's trek was so long that the following day we were once more immobilised in camp. Two horses were ill, we hadn't found replacements for the stolen pair, and the other nine were knackered. The honeymoon was over and the expedition had very suddenly taken on a serious face. With our eleven remaining horses, we had set out early hoping to reach a cache of supplies about twenty-five miles farther down the Haraa River. After four hours in the saddle, as we approached a small lumber town called Tunghil, Nikolai, Bazra and I cantered ahead to report the stolen horses to the police and try to wire a message to Hinton. We would catch up with the others on the far side of town and then hopefully stop for lunch and water the horses in the Haraa.

At a dusty, creaking little building housing Tunghil's post and telegraph station, we dismounted and tied our horses to a rail erected for the purpose. There was no sign on the building, but a rusting, unconnected satellite dish leaning on its side in the dirt seemed to point the way. Leaving Nikolai outside to guard the animals, Bazra and I went inside. None of the lights worked in the musty two-room building but the blank static of a small television screen provided a grey half-light to the tune of what sounded like a Chinese soap opera.

Sitting with her back to the door, transfixed by the flickering grey dots and zooming horizontal lines of the static, a burly Mongol woman was alone in the building. After twice being prodded by Bazra she turned around and gave us her best state employee's glare. Bazra growled something derogatory in Mongolian and reached past her and grabbed the telephone. He dialled a number a couple of times, then tried again and passed me the handset. I heard faint squeaks down the line, too faint for me to know if they were supposed to be intelligible, and then Bazra shouted into the receiver over the lap of the operator. She muttered and stroked her knuckles with hairy malice. The shouting finished, we emerged blinking into the glare of what had become a scorching afternoon. Nikolai and our tack had attracted the attention of eight rugged little boys just too young to be in school, if there was one. Like almost every Mongol we met, the boys were intrigued by the flat-topped pommel, square horn and cupped seat of our American cowboy saddles.

'Hey, Nik. Looks like you've been having fun out here. You're being treated like a rock star.'

'Sure', he said, looking at the little boys. 'If you call Michael Jackson a rock star.'

Nikolai hadn't seen John and the others. Bazra asked directions to the police station and we mounted up and rode a couple of hundred yards to the other end of town. At the police building Bazra dismounted and told us to wait outside. He went in to ask about our stolen horses. When he emerged grumbling five minutes later we assumed the worst and mounted up in silence.

After cantering and trotting a quarter of a mile past the last ger on the far side of town, we had still not seen any sign of our other companions. Before splitting up we had discussed two different routes we could take after Tunghil. Had they taken the wrong one? We should certainly have seen them by then if they had taken the same route as we had. After another quarter of a mile the horses began to tire.

'Bazra... where are Dorj and Enke?'

He looked at me, crinkled his eyes, rolled a cigarette, lit it and turned his horse around and kicked it into a trot back towards Tunghil. I should have asked earlier, but I had assumed that he would never have sent half the party off into the steppe without knowing where they were going. It was becoming clear that we couldn't rely on anything.

Next to a single ger just outside of town we pulled up beside a leathery old woman tending a cooking pot with her granddaughter and dog. Bazra asked if they had seen a bunch of riders and pack-horses go past. The woman pointed down the Haraa valley, identifying the alternative route to the one we had started to take.

We headed off in that direction, cursing the others as their path took us up and down steep, rocky ravines and through thick stands of alder. A mile later we emerged from the thickets into hilly, open country. After a couple more miles, Nik spied our friends through a pair of field glasses. They were on the far side of yet another big valley and by the time we had caught them up they had reached the bank of the Haraa and dismounted for lunch. When we arrived, the Gambler and Nyamdorj were asleep on the grass and their mounts were resting on their haunches, eating. Their pack-horse was lying on its side, too exhausted to continue. The re-supply point was still more than fifteen miles farther on. Bazra, Nikolai, John, Enke and I set off immediately, leaving the Gambler and Nyamdorj, their mounts, and their pack-horse in various states of proneness on the steppe.

Imperceptibly, the Haraa valley had widened out into a glorious sight. It was broad, curving, flat-floored and greener than any valley we had seen in Mongolia. At about seven o'clock we met a Mongol couple, each of them about nineteen years old. Their eyes were slitted against the glare and the wind, and under their dark nomadic complexions I saw the redness where the wind and the sun had burned deep. Exhausted, we sat down on the grass with them and rolled a cigarette high above the dark green valley. The boy smoked with us and pointed the way to our destination. It was about ten miles distant, on the far side of an arm of hills reaching down to the Haraa plain three valleys away. We and the horses had had a long day and those ten miles looked like twenty.

We set off down the hill on foot, pulling the horses behind us. Wide, lush, reddening in the evening light, the valley was beautiful but as the fierce steppe sun sank before us we had to tilt our hats down onto our noses and we didn't see much. There was no sign of the Gambler and Nyamdorj.

We chose a campsite in the ten o'clock dusk and Bazra took Nikolai's horse, a strong chestnut gelding, and rode off to pick up our supplies and inquire about fresh horses. An hour later we were falling asleep by the fire, so Nikolai, with the one sleeping bag that was not out wandering the steppe with the Gambler, crawled into our tent and slept. John and I kept the coffee simmering and checked the horses every twenty minutes. By one o'clock in the morning, with Bazra, the Gambler and Nyamdorj still absent, we were worried. We lit a candle and set up Bazra's tent for Enke, who had fallen asleep on a horse blanket by the fire.

At three o'clock that morning we noticed a horse where previously we had not counted one. Frightened, we ran through the numbers once more: thirteen to start with, two stolen makes eleven, one with Bazra and four with the Gambler and Nyamdorj makes six with us. We continued our count with a sudden, looming sense of fear. There were seven horses. Where had the seventh come from? Bazra? But the new horse was black, not the chestnut he had ridden away. It couldn't be that the Gambler and Nyamdorj had finally arrived, for they had four horses with them, not just one.

John and I crouched down in a thicket, shielding ourselves from the moonlight which came from just above the horizon and threw long shadows on the dewy prairie grass. We were tired and cold and our thoughts turned acutely towards the dramatic.

Bazra was angry and drunk, a couple of valleys away with his friend who had our supplies. The Gambler and Nyamdorj did not even know where our camp was. We had already lost two horses to thieves. We were alone on the edge of the wilderness and the only towns around were tough logging and prison settlements. People had seen us riding past with our many horses and our western saddles and full bags. Bazra says that every Mongol man has a gun somewhere in his ger. Unarmed strangers on the lawless steppe, we were vulnerable. Our remaining horses were spread out over a wide distance in the dark, and there was now a strange horse tethered to a tree on the edge of our pasture.

We scurried back to the fire and added fuel to the low coals until we had a good blaze. We hunkered down and brewed more coffee, squinting as the shifting wind chased us around the fire. After another three nervous checks, the horse was still there. Where was his rider?

We looked out into the dark for a while and then John got up to piss before turning in. I sat hunched by the fire, shaking with excess coffee and tobacco, nodding off stiffly in the cold.

'Hello! I am John!' I heard his voice ring out with unusual gusto and precision. I dragged myself from the fire and walked towards the voice. Three men rode up and dismounted. We took off our gloves and shook their hands. I held my left hand open and before me in a vaguely tribal gesture that I hoped would signify that I was friendly and unarmed.

Then Bazra rode into camp. He explained that the strangers were carrying our supplies, and asked me what I was doing wandering around at that time of night. We talked and he reminded me that the Gambler

25

and Nyamdorj had had one pack-horse with them, not two. There was something shaky, scratchy, unpredictable about him. John and I fell into fitful sleep by the fire, cold despite our wool hats and gloves and thick coats, snapping occasionally into consciousness under the hard stares of a drunk, surly Bazra and the three herdsmen.

When I awoke to a harsh, bright day, Bazra was still surly, the Gambler and Nyamdorj had not been heard from and were probably still shambling about the plains and valleys looking for us, and my tough little mare and Enke's grey gelding were coughing badly and hanging their heads low and listless.

Things were not good. Most of our horses were exhausted, ill, or missing and Bazra had been unable to find new ones. I drew him aside for a talk. He was almost twice my age. He was deep inside his own country, he was better with the horses, and his friends outnumbered mine. I had to be firm but he had the upper hand and, if anything went wrong, Nikolai, John and I would be very exposed indeed. But the expedition was grinding down far sooner than even the sceptics had feared and it was time to take charge, somehow.

Knowing the best hope was to make him respect us as men and to remind him of what he had felt when he had seen our cause as his, I tried to do the real talking with my eyes. I said he and I would have to start taking things more seriously. He stared nervously out at the steppe as I spoke. I moved into his field of vision and encouraged him to hold my gaze. 'We have to communicate better,' I said. 'We can't separate unless we know exactly where everybody is going.' I continued in that vein, trying to emphasise the 'we', to link him to the total commitment that John, Nik and I felt.

'Yes, Bull,' was all he said.

We spent the rest of the morning trying to get the practicalities back on track. Bazra and Enke cooked up a horse-cure with vodka, Bulgarian aspirin, and dandelions. We administered this unlikely restorative through a vodka bottle shoved up the horses' raised nostrils. The horses seemed to appreciate it, for the coughing soon stopped and they were lively enough when we rode on the next day. After lunch we sat in the shade, writing, mending our gear, waiting for Nyamdorj and the Gambler and hoping the dejected mood would pass. Nikolai threw a few casts into the Haraa from the river bank by camp.

Within three minutes he had caught a brace of handsome twelve-pound salmon, the first fish of the expedition. A cheer went up around the camp, the mood brightened palpably, and the hard glare of the day suddenly felt like a clear, dry warmth. Nikolai, John and I set off downstream, rods in hand.

When we returned to camp, Bazra had a visitor with him, a broad bull-faced man who wore a demeanour of hard benevolence and an opulent black-trimmed red del. On his head was the traditional pointed hat. I squatted about ten yards from Bazra and the stranger, whittling and making it clear that I was available if they wanted me. Bazra was too tightly wound to risk making him lose more face, so I was waiting for him to make the first move. I contented myself with knife and branch and with gazing at three beautiful horses, much stronger and sleeker of coat than our own, that were tethered to a nearby tree. After five minutes, Bazra called me over. He needed $190 to buy two horses from the silent herdsman, their owner.

He rode off to perform the transaction ritual in the herdsman's ger, presumably so he wouldn't have to share the booze with us. Nikolai, John and I had a major wash-up for the celebratory dinner in honour of the salmon and new horses. John found a gentle, swirling pool upstream, and I swam down the river for about a hundred yards, scraping along the rocks and sand-bars. We had a scrub-down in the cold water and then took photos in our smartest dinner dress: wool trousers, khaki shirts we had washed in the afternoon, and fresh bandanas.

Enke, smiling more than ever, cooked up a fish-head and potato soup and grilled the salmon, which we ate in big chunks with our hands. The flesh was firm and sweet, the best fish I have ever tasted. Half-way through dinner the Gambler and Nyamdorj rode into camp. Luckily they didn't like to eat fish.

chapter three

LEAN AND MEAN: FROM DURT TO THE SIBERIAN FRONTIER

8TH JUNE, THE STEPPE ABOUT FIVE MILES EAST OF THE HARAA RIVER

Nikolai caught another twelve-pound salmon for breakfast this morning. While Bazra, Nyamdorj and the Gambler appeared to be tending to the horses routinely, Nik, John and I broke down the camp. The Mongols were surly and hung-over and we didn't want to upset our remaining equilibrium by doing anything other than going about our business and letting them take care of theirs. After the saddle bags had been packed with food and rain gear, the bed-rolls strapped to the backs of our saddles, and the tent packed up, Enke told us that three horses had been stolen during the night. We were left with ten horses, eight of them healthy. It was bad news.

I looked around for Bazra. Nyamdorj was lying on his side on the rocky ground, drunk. The Gambler was shambling about, hunched and crazy-eyed. He wandered in and out of camp, appearing and reappearing from God knew where.

Nik, John and I decided that we'd had enough of these two. We didn't need them and we didn't have enough horses to carry them and their food. I called Bazra over and asked him what he knew of the missing horses and why he hadn't told us about them. He had a wild, hunted look, at once shifty, scared and indignant. The Gambler was looking for them, he said.

'Maybe tomorrow, maybe...'

'Forget about tomorrow,' I said. 'We're getting out of here and we're leaving the Gambler and Nyamdorj to sort out their own problems.'

I looked back as we trotted off. Nyamdorj was still prostrated on the ground and the Gambler was trotting away down the valley, searching for his brother's three horses. We rode about four miles, a scrappy little column of coughing horses and tense riders making their way towards the ger of a man Bazra said was brother to the President of the Republic. On the way, I pulled Bazra ahead of the pack for a talk.

'It's not your fault if Dorj [the Gambler] and Nyamdorj aren't capable of looking after the horses.' This was a lie. 'What is most important is that we communicate. Next time there is a problem, you must tell us immediately. If we are not confident that you are telling us everything, we will have to ask you many questions.' He didn't like questions.

'Maybe horses... tomorrow... today, come back. I did not do this thing. Maybe Dorj... Dorj, he is not a strong man. Maybe...'

'Thank you, Bazra.'

'This man we go to see now is very important man. Maybe from him or the other man we can get one more horse.'

We had started with thirteen horses. After having five stolen, buying two, and leaving one with the Gambler, we were left with nine. Two of these were ill. Seven horses for five riders, with provisions and equipment – it would not do. I looked back at Nik and John. They were

29

laughing with Enke. Bazra and I looked off at the far ridges a little longer and then I turned to him.

'Bazra, I think maybe we leave Enke in Durt. We have few horses, not healthy horses. Enke is a very good woman, very beautiful. But maybe too many people, not so many horses...' Bazra and Enke had recently been waking up in Bazra's tent together. Would he want to leave her behind?

He thought in silence for fifty yards.

'Maybe not so bad idea. Less people, faster. We free men. Bull, Bazra, Nik, John. Like this we ride fast. Maybe... I am thinking about it.'

A flash of strength charged Bazra's eyes for the first time in days. Streamline the party and charge north. Lean and mean, that was the way to do it. He was often talking about the 'real Mongol man', his independence and his love of the steppe and the mountains. I had hoped that leaving his new woman behind would galvanise him into this feeling of a new dawn for the expedition. It seemed to be working.

Half an hour later we came to Durt, where Bazra said the President's youngest brother lived. His ger smelled of mutton fat and tobacco smoke and did not in any way stand out from the fifteen others that constituted the village. Bazra and Enke stayed outside while we three went in. Our host, who spoke no English, bade us sit and we did so on the wood floor. He fed us wordlessly, moving calmly in a dark heat alleviated only by gusts of wind coming up through chinks in the uneven floor. First we ate bread, and then mutton and noodle soup. All the while I was hoping that out in the sunlight Bazra had the guts to tell Enke her time was up. Otherwise I would have to.

When we had shuddered down the last of the stew we thanked our host and emerged dazzled into the light of the day. We saw Bazra had done the right thing, saddled up, bid farewell to a weeping Enke, and rode off down the steppe.

Our next stop was the ger of the rich herdsman from whom we had bought the two horses. Bazra told us with great solemnity that the 'big gentleman' was 'the youngest brother of the President'. Two of these eminences in one day seemed like pretty good going. The second was encamped in a lone ger in a snaking and intensely green valley watered by a deep, narrow stream at which about sixty horses and cattle drank in groups of up to a dozen. Other livestock grazed along the valley.

We tied the horses to a corral and entered the ger. In the steppe you can enter any man's home as long as you don't knock on the door and don't step on the threshold. Our host was indeed the sturdy vizier from whom we had bought the two horses yesterday. He sat at a low central table. To his left sat his three stern children, all with the same hard demeanour. Nikolai, John, Bazra and I sat along the right-hand side of the table as new visitors should, our left knees and legs flat on the ground, our right knees propped up before us. Thus we showed our host that we concealed nothing dangerous in our laps.

The vodka emerged at two o'clock and our chances at a productive day disappeared therewith. Our host had bred several champion race horses, ridden to victory at Naadam, the annual national festival, by his eldest son. We admired the medals, the victory photographs and the heroic child, now thirteen and looking as tough as his father, and discussed a variety of horse-combs and other heirlooms passed down from the latter's great-great-grandfather. I asked our host about a photograph of a man standing in an office wearing a del. He said the man was his cousin, Ochirbat, President of the Republic.

10:30P.M., 9TH JUNE, ON THE WEST BANK OF THE SHARINGOL RIVER

We awoke to a bowl of fresh yogurt and a pair of fresh horses. We left one of our own sick animals behind and set off north into the mountains and southern forests of the Hentei range. By all accounts, we are the first foreigners to be going north to the border by the mountain route.

In the wooded foothills we passed a group of prisoners who had been sent, heads shaven, into the forest to harvest wild garlic, which is distributed by the government as a source of vitamin C in winter. We are taking special care of our equipment and horses tonight, a precaution that comes none too soon considering that we have already lost two grooms, five horses and a cook.

That said, things are in relatively good shape. Our smaller team is much sharper, the horses are healthier, and Bazra has regained his confidence. John has a sinister running infection in his left eye. He is clearly in some discomfort but is being typically game and claims to be proud to have achieved two-thirds of his ambition of being a back-woodsman half-blind and crazed with hooch. Now all he needs is some of Bazra's vodka.

We are composing the Tamerlane Blues to the tune of a blues riff from John's harmonica but the words are not suitable for this journal. Behind us a bird is singing with a high warble followed by a vomiting gurgle. The Mongols call it the go-to-bed bird.

9:30 P.M., 11TH JUNE, ON THE WAY TO THE YOROO RIVER

We covered a good twenty-five miles today and are camped in a very pretty alpine valley. It is catching the last light with a soft, dim rosiness and the horses are happy with their rich pasture in the crook of a small river. We see more flowers every day as the short spring matures and there is a sense of hurry about the beauty that we see all around us. The cold nights remind us how close the Mongols live to nature and explain much of their generosity with cream and yogurt and other fruits of the brief spring and summer.

The day's ride took us through the wooded mountains that make the Hentei region Mongolia's prime logging area. The logging appears to happen on a scale that is small, almost amateur, by international standards but which has nonetheless scarred the landscape in places. The uphill side of each of the mountain tracks is marked by vertical gashes of erosion that reach up to twenty feet in height. We have seen many old stumps, but nothing remotely like a clear-cut. At the one active site that we have passed, about twenty-five 30-foot logs of red spruce were being loaded onto a flat-bed lorry. A pair of trails led up a hillside into the woods, where the trees were selected and cut, and whence they were dragged down to be loaded and taken out of the mountains.

The tracks were covered with pine branches. In Sweden this practice is now being encouraged as a way of preventing erosion. We could not learn why it is being used here, but whatever the reason it limits damage to the land. We have also observed about a dozen hillsides marked with horizontal furrows, about eighteen inches wide and seven feet apart. Bazra says that these small trenches are dug to encourage the growth of red spruce.

We reckon that the furrows work by trapping seeds and channelling water to them. I suppose that the ultimate aim is to log the trees that grow up and, while we would rather not see logging take place in these wild mountains, it is encouraging to see a system that relies on natural processes. What I have seen of Mongolia in general and its logging practices in particular makes me doubt that anybody, Mongol or foreigner, will ever get around to logging the region seriously.

Bearing a bowl full of yogurt, Bazra has just returned from a visit to the family who live in this valley. We have clean clothes drying in the trees, a reasonable distance to cover tomorrow, fresh yogurt to send us on our way in the morning, and promises from John and Nikolai to rise early and have a go at the local trout. Venus is as usual the first light in the sky, followed by Mars and now by a growing population of lesser deities.

10:40 P.M., 13TH JUNE, EAST BANK OF THE YOROO RIVER
The Yoroo is a curving, slow river that has carved a flat valley about twelve miles wide. In this valley is Yoroo, a tough, dirty little collection of wooden shacks. We were met on the bridge coming in by a grizzled old scoundrel who showed an alarming interest in our knives, rifle and saddles. He smelled like the sort of man who knew where to find a drink. When we asked him who was selling he nominated himself.

We rode through several long valleys today, each time coming over a rise to see in front of us yet more of the vast, open, rolling plain. We stopped for lunch on a saddle of land in the middle of one of these valleys exactly six minutes after our first sighting of the Yoroo, which we had been searching for for three days. Later that afternoon we stopped at a ger to ask directions. We tied the horses to a corral and sat down outside to a plate of dried yogurt, its bitterness drowned in sweet, fresh clotted cream. Before the food came the ceremonial pinch of snuff.

We have about fifty miles to travel during the next few days. It sounds plausible and looks so on the map but we have learned not to be optimistic. Weather, horses and Bazra are an unpredictable combination. For the moment the horses are in decent shape. They are still coughing and mine and Bazra's have large girth-strap sores behind their forelegs but all are strong and looking much sleeker than at the start of the journey. Nikolai, in his first real test as our doctor, seems to have cured John's eye with antibiotics.

Around the breakfast fire the following morning we had a long talk about which of three possible routes we should take. Bazra insisted, as

usual, on reading the maps upside down. After twenty minutes of considering the various options we chose the one that seemed best, saddled up, and began to load the pack-horses. As we did so a pair of boys rode past on the way to their herds. Bazra spoke to them briefly and they disappeared down the river valley.

Soon enough we were mounted up and heading out of the valley. Bazra started to lead us in one of the directions we had rejected. Nikolai, John and I looked at each other but said nothing, hoping the new path was but a short-cut on the way to our chosen route. This became less and less likely and finally Bazra said 'I think maybe we take this route.'

'It looks like we're already taking this route.'

He was silent.

'Bazra, I thought we agreed on the other route.'

'I speaking to boys, I change my mind.'

'We've just spent twenty minutes making the opposite decision. Now you change your mind and don't tell us?'

'I think maybe this way okay.' He was probably right – the boys must have known the country intimately.

'What did the boys say about it?'

'Why so many questions? You ask so many questions.'

Back came that old edginess, banished so promisingly when we had dumped Enke, the Gambler and Nyamdorj and picked up fresh horses but a few days ago.

We carried on at a walk through that raw greyness so common on spring mornings in cold places. Bazra was talking nervously to himself. Gradually he seemed to wind down. After fifteen minutes of relative peace he cantered ahead of the pack and around the shoulder of a low, curving ridge. After a few minutes we caught him up. He was talking again and the nerves were back, worse than ever.

'Mongolian man free man. I real man. Always complaining. Always questions. I free man.' He repeated and repeated and repeated himself. The tone was provocative.

Nikolai saw me bridle. 'Don't,' he said. 'His world is closer to Sitting Bull's than Bartle Bull's – he doesn't understand you. Don't push him over the edge.'

John agreed. I paused and looked at Nik. He clearly meant what he was saying. I respected his instincts and level head and thought he was more likely to be right than I was.

'No problem, Bazra. Everything okay.'

This calmed him down for a minute or two, but he still had that wild look in his eye. He started laughing shakily and took to raving anew.

'Ah, Bull,' he said, leaning into me. 'You angry with me.' I smelled his

34

breath; he was drunk. He unslung his rifle.

'John, you my friend. My best friend.'

He handed John the rifle.

'Please John, my friend, you kill me.'

John, prudent Yankee that he is, declined.

When we came to a fork in the valley we had to make another decision. I suggested we dismount and smoke. Bazra eased down another notch and smoked in silence until something re-lit his fire and he took up his rifle and leapt to his feet. Those thin, steppe-seared eyes blazed as, gun in hand, he soared off on a soliloquy addressing the respective merits of shooting the beautiful American boys, shooting himself, or riding off for a few months' sport in the Hentei Mountains. His own freedom, the freedom of Mongol men generally, and his disdain for money, Americans and fear were other prominent themes.

There was nothing for it but to roll another round of smokes. John offered one to Bazra. It shut him up again and after a few minutes of intense consultation of map and compass we mounted up and rode on. Nik and John held back as we rode up the next valley. I talked to Bazra about the wildlife, the weather and his children. His eldest boy was called Temujin, which was Genghis' name before he became khan.

All seemed good and calm until John and Nik trotted up and suggested a round of 'Rawhide'. We had forgotten the effect that this song invariably had on the horses. They broke into a trot, the pace rising gradually until Bazra started whipping every horse in reach into a canter and then a gallop. His pack-horse collapsed, somehow performing a full somersault in the dust. Bazra dragged the animal to its feet and off we went again until the horses tired and we settled into a walk.

At the head of the valley, after a long and gentle ascent from its wide floor, we stopped for lunch. The sun, given a chance at last, had burned away the ground-hugging shroud of damp and the grey morning was now a bright day. Before us the valley head became a rounded pass where two lines of hills met. On the far side, we hoped, a new valley would begin. This we would follow down and northwards to the Tojeenars Forest, the last big landmark between us and Siberia.

Behind us, opening out and downwards in a huge green fan, was the country we'd just covered. We could see clear to the farthest horizon we'd yet seen. The view was magnificent in that limpid prairie sunlight, as vast and eternal a landscape as any on earth. The narrow juncture of the hills behind us protected us from the northerly wind and with the sun overhead we felt warm for the first time we could remember. Time, a gallop and the view had cured our free Mongolian friend and for all of us the lunch seemed far more than salted mutton and pickled cabbage.

Opposite:
Tying up the horses
for the night
(J.B.)

In almost the very centre of the day's last valley, more a huge undu-
lating bowl than a valley, we spotted the lonely whitish dot of a ger.
There were no horses outside and no smoke rose from the chimney. Nor
could we see any other sign of anybody being around. We hobbled a few
of our horses, tied the rest to the rails of a small corral and stepped
inside. Stooping low under the door frame, we entered a space so dark
that at first we could hardly see. An old man sat cross-legged at the far
end, smoking a long silver pipe. Its bowl glowed a low red in the gloom.
We crossed our legs on the felt floor and sat in silence for a few minutes.
The old man acknowledged us each with a nod of his head and we rolled
some smokes. He passed Nikolai a stone snuff bottle and one by one we
tapped it against the fleshy join of thumb and forefinger on our left
hands. The bottle was empty. Bazra handed over his own snuff bottle
and the old herdsman tipped out a bit for himself. They spoke quietly
for four or five minutes and we took our leave.

We mounted up and rode on towards the end of the great circular valley, pleased to have the sun at our backs as we headed north. About six
miles on, the bowl rose up to a brief shelf before the Tojeenars Forest,
hundreds of square miles of cedars and conifers rooted in flat, sandy
soil. On the edge of the forest we made camp. We had seen a couple
more gers in far fingers of the valleys and we'd been warned that a bear
had taken some livestock a few days ago, and there were wolves about,
so we proposed taking turns on a night watch. No worries, said Bazra,
insisting he would spend the night among the horses.

Three groups of teenaged boys, about ten in all, rode up and joined
our fire before we turned in. They were a tough, swaggering bunch. On
their heads they wore a collection of rather assertive adornments: a
piratical head-scarf, a Dudayev fedora, a black leather Gestapo number,
a couple of army-issue khaki baseball hats and a few versions of the
more traditional Mongol trilby. Each of the boys sat his saddle cocked
sideways in an exaggerated slouch. Several of them didn't dismount.
They just sat their horses on the fringe of the firelight for ten minutes or
so, slumped over with their forearms crossed on their mounts' withers,
watching us in silence and then cantering away.

I can still picture a few of the horses. It might have been the firelight
or maybe it was the hard silence of their riders, but those horses seemed
the biggest and strongest we had seen in Mongolia. Although his front
end was all I saw of him by the light of our fire, I remember one in
particular, a brick-jawed broad-chested grey with a neck that spread
straight from head to forelegs in a fearsome cannon of muscle.

After the last group of boys had ridden off, presenting us with a bowl
of dried yoghurt before they mounted up, we checked our horses and

turned in. Bazra was adamant about watching the horses himself and took personally any further suggestions of a watch. John shared a quiet last smoke with him and then joined Nikolai and me at the fire. We listened to a couple of wolves howling from the forest as we lay in our bags looking up at the night sky. There wasn't much of a moon and overhead the stars shone with uncanny clarity, so abundant and seemingly so close that if we'd had more pack-horses I might have plucked a couple and taken them north with us. Oh well, I thought as I drifted off, they'll be wherever we're going.

Opposite:
Nikolai and the author,
Suchbaatar
(J.B.)

We awoke to a frosty morning and another stolen horse. He was a useful little black gelding but we took it philosophically. If we'd lost that horse a few days earlier it would have been trouble, but the timing meant it was Bazra's problem and not ours. We had only fifty miles or so to go, maybe two days' ride or three at the worst. Our numbers were leaner than they had been, the remaining horses were finally healthy and we'd eaten most of the food that earlier on composed most of the pack-horses' burden. From our point of view we had one fewer horse to drag. From Bazra's point of view a pretty awful homecoming was waiting in a green valley south-west of Ulan Bator.

After a long day's ride we emerged from the far margin of the Tojeenars Forest. We rode up onto a rise and our northern horizon was Siberia. We let out a weary cheer and took turns savouring the sight through John's field glasses. There it was, broad and flat and grassy, looking no different from Mongolia but set apart by the thin thread of the border fence rising and dipping across the prairie.

We could just discern the town of Kiakhta, namesake of a 1727 treaty which had for the first time in history closed that long border to the horsemen of the steppe. The Treaty of Kiakhta had not only formalised most of the Sino-Russian border but also ceded Mongolia to China and opened the Chinese market to the legal importation of Russian furs. This vast new market for Siberia's pelt harvest was to provide the final fuel for Russia's exploration and conquest of northern Asia. As Siberia yielded her last sable grounds to the Slavic invasion, Chinese demand for the skins of sea otters and other mammals brought Russians into the North Pacific and ultimately down the coast of Alaska.

China's insistence that the border crossing be located at Kiakhta was considered baffling by contemporaries and remains a mystery to modern historians. The closest drinking water was half an hour distant and firewood had to be carted from twenty miles away. An English traveller called Captain John Cochrane, who walked across Siberia in the early 1820s, wrote that Kiakhta had 'soil so poor that even common vegetables are with great difficulty raised'. From our vantage point on that

June day almost two centuries later, it certainly looked a forlorn place to choose as one of the most important points on earth for communication between the two worlds of East and West.

A staggering amount of trade crossed that desolate border in the late eighteenth century. In a good year up to ten thousand carts bearing Chinese goods would pass through on their way to Irkutsk, Siberia's administrative capital and principal entrepot. A million chests of tea, more than a million yards of Chinese cotton and twenty-five tons of rhubarb and other dried medicinal roots entered Russia annually through Kiakhta. In return eight million Siberian pelts would pass the other way. Not until the opening of the Chinese treaty ports in the 1830s and 1840s would that lonely valley begin to slide back into obscurity.

Opposite:
'Nations comprising
The Russian Empire'

The current border crossing is fifteen miles to the south-west, between the Mongolian town of Suchbaatar and a smaller Russian settlement called Naushki. We turned west along the Yoroo valley and headed for Suchbaatar, saying goodbye to the ghosts of Kiakhta's traders, customs men, cartwrights and innkeepers. Using wood we had collected in the Tojeenars Forest, we made our final Mongolian campfire about ten miles west of Suchbaatar. Then we settled in to the task of making sure Bazra wouldn't have too much vodka to weigh him down on the return trip. We had as good as made it to the first major milestone of an expedition that promised to last at least another three months.

The only way to cross the border was on a brief stretch of the old Trans-Siberian railway spur that runs from Irkutsk across Mongolia to Beijing. When we rode into Suchbaatar we found there were no trains that day, so we tied the horses to trees outside the main hotel and checked in, very pleased to see that our friend Hinton was there to meet us. As we said farewell to Bazra, who had met up with a couple of 'brothers' who were to help him with the ride back south, I fought a ghastly feeling that the poor man was doomed to a rather hideous return. He was starting with a depleted herd of eight horses and the attrition along the trail was bound to be severe. His reception at the ger of the Gambler's brother would be even worse.

Carousing through the night with a flock of local tarts, a team of Mongol wrestlers occupied the rooms around us. These men were huge, bruised and very drunk. An ungodly variety of noises ensured that despite our firmly locked door we didn't sleep much. In the morning, we boarded the train for the brief hop into Russia.

A well-dressed Mongol couple, both about sixty years old, drew the short straw in the seat allocation stakes and spent the next hour and a half sharing their train cabin with the saddles, tents, sleeping bags and men of the Tamerlane Expedition. They were academics of some sort and both spoke good English, so I asked them for translations of the names of some of the flora we had seen on the trail north. 'Artemisia', she said of one flower. 'Artemisia vulgaris – because there are so many at this time of year.' With this, and despite her beatific smile, it occurred to me that she was not the sort of woman to relish asphyxiation by horse stench and human body odour.

After ten minutes of scribbling I fell asleep as the border fence approached across the green middle distance.

Народы обитающіе въ россійской Имперіи.
Nations composant l'Empire Russe.

THE BOUNDARY POST.

They have marched away into Siberia

chapter four

THE AUTONOMOUS REPUBLIC OF BURYATIA

AN hour later I awoke to a prod in the ribs from a downy-chinned Russian conscript. The train had travelled the three miles from the border post to the Naushki station and it was Russian customs-and-immigration time. As John, Nikolai and I groped for our documents the soldier poked around in our kit. He raised his eyebrows at the second saddle that he saw and looked at me quizzically upon discovering the third. He looked more closely at our attire, took note of the cowboy hats on our laps and knees, and realised we weren't typical travellers. The Mongol woman in our cabin told him something explanatory in Russian and he left the cabin.

Opposite:
'The Boundary Post' welcomed hundreds of thousands of exiles and convicts into Siberia

He returned with another private and an officer. Trouble? I reached for our letters from Mikhail Gorbachev and the Council of American Ambassadors. Nikolai nudged me and I looked up to see the soldiers playing with our hats and saddles and laughing. 'Cowboys, yes? Marlboro Man *ochin harasho* [very good]!' We gave the privates our passports and visas. The mirth left their faces and they passed the documents on to their officer, pointing at something. He frowned and showed me my visa. It was written in Cyrillic script and I had no idea what it said. I was able to offer only my best Gallic shrug in reply. The Mongolian woman, looking over my shoulder, explained that 'Moscow' had been put down as our point of entry. Moscow was three thousand miles away. The officer looked at us again, scratched his chin, and broke back into a smile. 'American cowboys OK,' he said, and led his men from the cabin.

'There was a time when it was easier to get into Siberia,' I said to nobody in particular when the soldiers had gone.

'Certainly,' said the Mongol woman. 'The state would facilitate your arrival like the most honoured guest. You would be so welcome that they would take offence if you tried to go home!' Indeed. In the old days the spring thaws would reveal the corpses of hundreds of convicts who had frozen to death trying to escape this land. Like the little yellow flowers that announce springtime in the taiga, the cadavers were called 'snow drops'.

An hour later, after the soldiers had been through the entire train, the doors at the ends of the various carriages were thrown open and we were allowed out into Russia. Too tired to care that we could as easily be there a week as an hour, we piled our saddles and bags in the shade of a tree on the platform and sat down on a nearby bench to await our friends. The western faces milling around among the Mongols and Buryats, the stands of merchants selling candy bars and Chinese sandals

43

and the wooden architecture of the station all drove home the feeling that we were in a place very different from Mongolia.

A cool southerly breeze blew along the platform, rustling the shade trees overhead and making specks of sunlight dance about in the shadows at our feet. The atmosphere had a cheery marketplace hum to it and the air was brisk and dry. Friends and relatives were greeting each other and nobody seemed to be saying good-bye. It was springtime in a place that waits a long time for the winter to end.

And step one of my dream had worked. We were on time and healthy and we'd done our job. It was a good moment and now there was nothing for it but to sit back and await the others. Nik handed me a beer he'd bought from one of the hawkers. I rolled it along my forehead to feel its chill. I cracked the can open, rolled a smoke, lit it, and sat back to let the moment happen.

We had been waiting for half an hour when a tall man leaned down in front of John and examined his face closely. I glanced at the stranger briefly, assumed he was mad and tried to ignore him. I watched John return his stare staunchly for a few seconds from beneath the wide brim of his hat. And then John leapt from the bench and simultaneously they cried out.

'Boit!'

'Taran!'

And then, together, 'You made it!'

I was wrong to think the man was a stranger but right to think he was mad. He was our expedition colleague and dear old friend Taran Davies, almost on time for once in his life. It was no wonder that we hadn't recognised each other. Taran had had his shoulder-length hair chopped off and John looked like the jilted, homicidal Klondiker in Service's 'The Shooting of Dan McGrew', 'a miner fresh from the creeks, dog-dirty, and loaded for bear'. Kerim Yalman, our fifth-core member, soon arrived with Dr Yukhnin of the Russian Academy of Sciences. A robust, hawk-nosed man with an invigorating air of confidence, Yukhnin grabbed my shoulders and straightened my back.

'Guys so small.' He whacked me on the upper arm. 'Why so small? You look like veemen.' From the look on his face he could have meant 'vermin'.

'We've just ridden half way across Mongolia, Doctor.'

'Guys need Russian food.' He rolled that R like an old Cold War bogeyman.

'Lake Baikal very big, you so small.' Whack. 'Tonight, I cooking dinner. Maybe little drinking.' Thump. 'Ve make you strong like Russian man.'

'Yes, Doctor.'

I turned to Kerim.

'KY!'

'Bull!'

'What brings you to Naushki?'

'I was worried you boys couldn't look after yourselves.'

He grabbed my saddle and with an armful of gear each we all walked out of the station and loaded the battered old military van that was to take us out of Naushki to our Russian base camp.

Before setting off, Yukhnin marched us into the station restaurant. It was empty save for two drunk Buryats in a corner and a sole Russian waitress. She had clearly been a star student in Seminar A: Surliness and Body-building, which every traveller knows to be a required part of the official syllabus for female employees of Slavic governments. After a couple of minutes she came to our table, planted her fists on the viscose-swathed buttresses that were her hips and gave Yukhnin a good hard stare. The Doctor, brave soul, said we'd like something to eat. Outrage replaced her 'try me if you dare' look and she looked at Yukhnin as if he'd just announced that he was a pederast.

'No food. The kitchen is shut.' Yukhnin pointed out gently that from our table we could see two cooks cooking in the kitchen. She ground her fists deeper into those medieval hips. Yukhnin tried a new approach, Party-bred sternness spiced with a roguish wink. She threw three oily menus on the table and sat down nearby for a smoke. Having thoroughly punished her cigarette, she returned to take our orders. Kerim had been translating the menu to the rest of us, but the Doctor stopped him. The waitress propped her pad on her dreadnought bosom and Yukhnin explained that Nik, John and I wanted the whole menu. Each. And some soup and bread for him, Kerim and Taran.

As the Mongolian veterans ploughed through dumplings, cabbage soup, vinyl schnitzels, watery beets and other savouries, Taran and Kerim talked us through their path to Naushki. Their last few weeks made our ride through Mongolia seem like lunch at Claridge's. They had overcome last-minute fund-raising crises, juggled two pairs of divorced parents in the crowds and humid June heat of a Harvard graduation, ventured unauthorised into the deepest bowels of Moscow's Sheremetyevo airport to find lost baggage, faced down skinheads on the back streets of Irkutsk and survived three quite senior Russian drinking sessions.

After forty minutes of jolting over the bumpy grassland of southern Buryatia in a south-easterly direction that took us back to the Mongolian border, the old green van groaned to a halt and we piled out. On a stretch of flat land in the crook of a bend in the Selenge, it seemed a well-chosen spot in which to spend the next two days resting, waiting for our horses and settling the upcoming logistics with Dr Yukhnin before he returned to Moscow. The Selenge flowed wide and brown in a serpentine path across the flat steppeland, the grass was thick, and a high butte behind camp lent drama in the otherwise gently rolling prairie that surrounded us.

Opposite:
The author and
Dr. Yukhnin at
Camp Selenge
(K.Y.)

In camp I had a chance to get a bearing on the two other Russian members of the expedition team who had come to Naushki with Kerim and Taran. Yukhnin re-introduced me to Oleg Massalski, indicating that he was a big cheese and required, wink-wink, extra respect. Massalski was a chain-smoking, weedy-looking sort with a pot-bellied expression that belied his powerful position in the region. He wouldn't be riding with us but, as the man in charge of an extensive state field infrastructure related to the study of seismology, he had access to the equipment, commodities and people that mattered. He was an old friend of Yukhnin's and a colleague from the Russian Academy of Sciences. His help with planning and logistics was an important part of that institution's sponsorship of our project.

Sergei Rasputin was to be our translator and a spare hand. A burly, fit twenty-seven-year-old, he had that combination of open face, fair features and calm, confident demeanour which always wins trust upon the first encounter. He had once spent a summer in Kansas, and his English was good.

His father, Valentin Rasputin, was Siberia's pre-eminent cultural figure. In his writings – mainly stories and essays defending Siberia's ecology and traditional culture – words like 'motherland' and 'patriotism' occur frequently. His patriotism was of an earthy, atavistic sort that is peculiarly Russian. He was an Old Believer of the secular age: an outspoken mystic with a ferocious spiritual attachment to the traditional Russia of ploughs, axes and bearded village wisdom. Such men, and the last Csar and his family thought they had found one in the unrelated Grigoriy Rasputin, speak to a part of Russians where gloom and suspicion reside alongside the sublime.

The last two Russian members of the field team had not yet arrived at camp. One of them, Yevgeny Kondratjev, was to be in charge of the horses. 'He is best horseman in Siberia. Very strong. Very honest. Good specialist,' said Yukhnin as he explained that Kondratjev was at a nearby collective farm choosing and rounding up the animals that would take us to and, God willing, around Baikal. Piotr Lobanov, our guide, was still in Irkutsk.

'Irkutsk, Doctor?' Up loomed the ghoulish spectre of another Bazra, of more maybes and *mañana*-land.

'Personal business.'

'He has had a year to do his personal business.'

'Guys! Piotr Lobanov is experienced hunter. Very good guide. He is coming.'

Shortly after lunch the next day, a thirty-foot cattle lorry came grinding over the steppe. It pulled up under a tree twenty yards from our fire and a man eased himself down from the passenger seat. The man must be Kondratjev. I could hear the horses knocking about in the lorry. He glanced in our direction, muttered something to himself, spat his cigarette on the ground, lit another and headed for the back of the lorry. He had a huge belly and the arse of a Clydesdale. His face was round and his eyes drooped downwards as if they'd had enough. He wore a light blue shirt with a flowery print, untucked. He was shod in rubber-soled espadrilles.

We had been expecting the Marlboro Man and instead we seemed to have a Torquay ice-cream salesman. I looked at Yukhnin with my eyebrows raised. He gave me a slightly alarmed look back and together we walked to the lorry. Yukhnin and Kondratjev introduced themselves.

'Welcome,' I said. Yukhnin translated this and Kondratjev turned to me with a wide smile. He was missing a tooth but his eyes were clear as a mountain stream.

'Genia,' he said, offering a fleshy palm. His handshake was strong and for a moment we held each other's gaze. Genia Kondratjev was no ice-cream vendor.

We unloaded the horses and walked them to the river's edge, where they all drank healthily. Rented from a nearby collective farm, they were much bigger than our Mongol horses. When the horses had been tethered in long grass on the river bank downstream from camp, Taran, Kerim, Nik, John and I walked among them, having a closer look. Genia joined us and pointed to one of the stallions. He wasn't the tallest but he was by far the broadest. His muscles stood out as if sculpted and his mane had been cut into a fearsome Mohican. He pulled at his tether and exuded an alert, aggressive energy, holding his head high when he wasn't eating. John christened him Sarge.

That night was our official send-off dinner. We were to hit the trail the following morning, with Yukhnin and Massalski returning to Irkutsk in the van. The great occasion was celebrated in suitably strong style. Called upon to make the first toast, I drank to the arrival of Genia and of the horses that we hoped would take us north to Baikal and all the way around it. Genia responded with a toast to me, announcing that I must be the one to ride the horse John had christened Sarge. Kerim drank to Massalski, Taran drank to 'our new Russian friends', and then

I lost track. Poor Sergei was having a difficult time translating all the nonsense being proposed, which must have seemed especially ridiculous to him as he was teetotal.

After the fifth or sixth toast I was concentrating so hard on maintaining equilibrium that all I could do was sit straight up, say as little as possible, and try to look serious. The huge effort of doing so gave me a stern demeanour which impressed Yukhnin. 'Bartle, very strong drinking.' He thrust his jaw forward, pursed his lips and gave me a thumbs up.

'Strong man,' said the Doctor. Little did he know. 'Here.' He splashed three fingers of vodka into my mug. 'Have more.'

By the time we rose to move to the fire nobody had proposed a toast to Yukhnin himself. Considering that enough toasts had been drunk to honour every man in Christendom the omission was rather embarrassing. Undeterred, Yukhnin was warming into the full glow of Slavic heartiness and he led Taran, John, Nik and me in a swim to camp from a hundred yards upstream. Kerim, meanwhile, had been lost to sweet dreams of harems and magic carpets on the grass in front of our tents.

After the swim we found some scotch in Nikolai's bag, watched Taran pass out by the fire, and drank the Doctor's health. We did it loudly and Yukhnin was pleased. As Nikolai and I got up to check the horses he waylaid us with great crunching bear-hugs. He made us trade punches to the gut with him and then arranged a wrestling match between Nikolai and the driver of the van.

Nik won emphatically, having applied all the delicacy of Tamerlane himself. We counted the horses and checked their tethers and returned to the fire. Another bottle of vodka was opened and that was the end of my night.

I awoke by the damp coals to a rather groggy international team of scientists and explorers. One of the tents was collapsed, clothes and boots were scattered round and flies were buzzing about a couple of puddles of vomit. The driver's face was covered with bloody mementoes of his waltz with Nikolai and the rest of us looked little better. Yukhnin, miraculously, was as hearty as the night before and sober enough to make the sensible suggestion that we might want another day in camp to 'prepare the equipment' for the ride ahead. I agreed, adding that the horses might want some more rest after their journey. God forbid that we should fail to ride because half the team was cross-eyed and the other half couldn't walk.

We broke camp early the next morning. Piotr Lobanov, our supposed guide, had not arrived. The boys chose their horses, I introduced myself to Sarge, and we saddled up. It was a powerful moment for us all, the first day of several months of mounting up and hitting the trail in

Russia, and the first ride with our full complement of the five core Tamerlane men: Nikolai, John, Kerim, Taran and me.

We rode about three miles along the Selenge before Genia led us down through marshy ground into a twenty-yard channel between the river bank and a low scrub-covered island. On the far side of the island, facing the far bank of the Selenge across a hundred yards of water, we came to a sandy beach that had been one end of a ferry crossing in the days before that level of civil society in Siberia had crumbled with the Soviet dream.

Opposite:
Genia after the Camp
Selenge massacre
(K.Y.)

Now we had to cross the Selenge. The river was wide and swift, we didn't know our new horses, and they were not comfortable with us. Taran and Kerim were inexperienced horsemen and Sergei had never ridden in his life. There was no way we could swim it on horseback. But Yukhnin had a plan. He had arranged for two local cowboys to await us on the far bank so that their horses, cleverly including a mare, could serve as bait or beacon to ours. We would drive our horses into the water and hope that they could be convinced to brave the current to reach the other horses on the far bank.

The law of the path of least resistance means that such an operation can only work if the horses are convinced that they must either cross or drown. Which means that if we couldn't prevent the horses from turning back to our shore the whole thing would collapse. We cut long poles from saplings by the beach, filled our trouser pockets with rocks of throwing size and removed our shirts for the charge into the water.

When all were present, armed and ready, a count of three would be the signal for us to burst into the loudest hullabaloo in all of Buryatia. We would accompany the shouting with sticks and slaps and rocks to drive the horses as far into the water as possible. We would then set up a line of noise and pole-thrashed white water along the bank to discourage any turning back.

I was tying my shoe laces when I heard Genia shouting in Russian. Worried that someone was hurt, I looked up to see that he had done away with the count of three and was running among the horses, hollering furiously and thrashing about with his pole. Men and animals charged into the water in an almighty chaos of whinnying and splashing and yelling. The first two or three horses swam out straight and true for the far bank. A couple more started to swim back to shore but we turned them around. And, in an ominous start to what was to be a long summer and autumn of river crossings, half of the horses turned back, flanked us or charged straight through us and into the bush.

We spent the next seven hours scouring the 80-acre island for traces of the horses, tracking them, chasing them and rounding them up on

foot and horseback. The island was an ungodly tangle of bogs and thickets, so labyrinthine that in its depths if you couldn't remember your way in it was hard to get out. By eight o'clock that evening, when the last horse had been roped, my hands, arms and face were striped with cuts but Sarge and I had enjoyed several thunderous gallops chasing our prey through the maze.

On the far bank we bought a lamb from a local herdsman, slaughtered it, and gorged ourselves in the long twilight of a northern mid-summer evening. Three drunk Buryats joined our fire, making nuisances of themselves. One of the Russian cowboys who had helped us with the crossing silenced the loudest of them with two crisp rights to the jaw and they rode off into the night.

Within a few days it had become clear that this grubby incident was not unusual in the Autonomous Republic of Buryatia. Buryatia is home to just over half of Russia's four hundred thousand Buryats. A Mongol people pushed north into the forests around Baikal by turbulence on the steppe in the tenth century, they are Siberia's largest indigenous nationality. Studying their story, one sees that the long and bloody Russian conquest of Siberia had much in common with the American expansion west: the pursuit of furs bringing Europeans ever deeper into a vast

continent of forest and plain, the establishment of garrisons and the consequent expansion of the state, an escalation from occasional bloodshed into intense local wars, the inevitable victory of European military technology, the ultimate subjugation of the original inhabitants, the gradual degradation of their cultures, continued tensions in the current era and the lingering subconscious guilt of a conquered land.

Of the many tribes and peoples whom the Russians conquered in their bloody drive to the Pacific, the Buryats had been the most formidable. Full-blooded Mongols, sharing in the traditional military strengths of their people – disciplined cavalry tactics, highly effective use of the bow and arrow, efficient communication – the Buryats resisted the Slavic advance for fifty years after the first clashes west of Lake Baikal. In the 1690s, the so-called Eastern Buryats of the Selenge Valley were the last to succumb to the Russians and their firearms.

Yasak, the tribute paid in furs that the Russians had imposed upon the tribes of Central Siberia in the late sixteenth and early seventeenth centuries, was the prime motivation behind the subjugation of the Buryats in Eastern Siberia during the latter 1600s. In 1646 the following threat had failed to deter Buryat resistance:

But if in future you rebels betray the Csar and do not hand over the Csar's yasak annually, and if you come to attack our fort and our peasant farmers, then for your treachery our leaders will send many of the Csar's soldiers with firearms to attack you, and they will command that not only you and your cattle, but your wives and children and all your people be killed and destroyed and your homes burned down mercilessly...[1]

Propagandists of the Soviet era had preferred to see this malign colonial history in the light of class liberation and Muscovite enlightenment. One of them wrote in the 1956 revisionist history *Narody sibiri* that

The voluntary union with the Russian state of various tribes and peoples of Siberia languishing under the oppression of the warring feudal nomadic lords of Asia answered the vital interests of the popular masses, including the Buryats. It delivered them from devastating feudal conflicts... and acquainted them with higher forms of economy, everyday life and culture.[2]

As we rode north to Lake Baikal through the steppe and forest of southern Buryatia, the legacy of Leninist 'Nationalities Policy' was obvious all around us, a second layer of tribal bleakness on top of that imposed by the original conquest. In further imperialist strife under Stalin, ten thousand Buryats were killed and nearly all of Buryatia's

Opposite:
A Buryat tending his herd, circa 1948

53

Buddhist temples were destroyed. Collectivisation, de-nomadisation, and the Russification of language and culture had enervated the indigenous people. The resulting despair and alcoholism were reminiscent of indigenous communities I have seen in Australia and North America.

After a few days of riding north through the Buryat steppe, during which we saw one isolated village and a couple of abandoned log cabins but no gers, we celebrated Mid-Summer's Night with a special fry-up of fresh mutton and potatoes, preceded by mutton-and-beet soup, with Swiss chocolate for pudding. Kerim had given me my first haircut of the journey before dinner and for the solstice feast itself we all bathed in a stream and wore our cleanest clothes. It was an idyllic evening as we sat out after dinner, toasting the year's longest day with a small whisky each.

The following afternoon we reached the top of a gentle hill and saw below us, stretching northwards, a long valley sprinkled at its near end with aspen. Farther down the valley the trees thickened into the distance until ultimately an uninterrupted sea of dark green forest reached to the horizon. Genia saw the view and bellowed with delight. 'A-guys, guys, taiga! Taiga!'

We had arrived at the southerly fringe of the taiga, the vast primeval forest which covers most of Russia. Marshy, largely coniferous, teeming with a fauna that includes the fur-bearing mammals which originally brought Russians over the Urals and into Asia, it stretches from the Baltic to the Pacific, running longitudinally between the grasslands of the south and the tundra of the far north. It is as close to the hearts of Russians as all the brown bear and Orthodox icons and every drop of vodka in their whole huge land. Due north, in the heart of this dark forest, lay Lake Baikal, the Sacred Sea of Siberia.

When we reached the bottom of the hill, when our horses stood upon the very threshold of the taiga, Genia dismounted. He insisted that we join him. Together, we wiped our feet before riding out of the steppe, 'that damned desert', as Genia called it, and into the hearth of Mother Russia.

11:25 P.M., 23RD JUNE, ON THE EAST BANK OF THE TEMNIK RIVER

After an eighteen-mile ride along a dirt logging road through thick taiga, we are camped in a grassy valley with a river called the Temnik flowing past us. Broad and shallow, flanked by evergreen-covered ridges, it is the picture of a Patagonia trout stream.

As of yesterday's threshold ceremony, we are in the taiga. We shall be in it through the autumn, covering a thousand miles, so we'd better get used to it. Sergei, with his cool, solemn demeanour, has been teaching us some of the wisdom of Siberian hunters. He is an urbanite, more an Irkutsk bourgeois than a taiga man like Genia. But he shares his father's reverence for the old Siberian grit.

Wryly but with respect, he has laid down 'The Teachings of Taiga': Never part with your spoon; never use matches to light a cigarette when you are by a fire; don't spit in the fire; never leave a trail to take a short-cut through the bush; when you are eating among friends, guard your own portion. At the table, says Sergei, you can trust strangers but not your friends.

About eight miles before camp yesterday, we crossed an old wooden bridge over a nameless river and saw upstream a dozen teenage girls splashing about in the water. 'Promising', said Taran. Twenty yards after the bridge, the forest opened out into a field in which a middle-aged couple and ten young men were lounging about a camp. Less promising. It was a school group and the girls were doing the washing. 'This', said Sergei, 'is the division of labour in a socialist utopia'.

We rode through what we expect is a typical Siberian village: dusty garbage-strewn dirt streets lined with wooden houses, shabby but for whimsical carvings, painted in cheery primary colours, above the doors and windows. We stopped to negotiate with a young Buryat for the purchase of six loaves of bread before pushing on. Our way took us down a long, flat valley densely carpeted with dandelions. Through this yellow froth Nik, John, Genia and I had a long canter so sublime that with some nice sugary music it could have been a perfume advert.

After an hour on the trail this morning, we found Dr Yukhnin and the long-awaited Piotr Lobanov waiting by the roadside with the van and the big old lorry, driven by Nikolai's wrestling opponent from the night of the Camp Selenge Massacre.

Piotr has shown signs of being a good cook and camp organiser. Let us hope he is as useful in the field. Yukhnin, who was in typically ebullient form, has shot off to Irkutsk. We expect to see him there in early July.

From Dr Yukhnin's vehicle, we collected the presents that we had brought from America to give to our Russian colleagues. Genia, Sergei and Piotr, who are riding with us, got first-rate sleeping bags identical to our own. For anybody who spends time in the bush where nights are cold, the quality of sleeping bags makes a huge difference: the good ones are lighter and warmer, dry more quickly, and retain heat better when wet, than the bad ones. Sergei was so delighted that for once we did not suspect irony in his voice when he told us he had always wanted a really good American sleeping bag. Genia was equally pleased, saying he would remember us when he was checking his traps alone this winter.

We also gave them each a sponge bag full of useful little things that we had been told could be hard to find in Siberia: razors, aspirin, vitamins, soap, toothpaste, antiseptic ointment. Piotr magnanimously said that if we wanted them to smell and look good we had better do the same ourselves. I was about to explain to Piotr that if he didn't want to put his toothbrush in his mouth he could put it somewhere even smellier, but a look from Nikolai shut me up. For Dr Yukhnin, who had organised the whole thing, we had brought a watch, a good one. He was elated and said that he had long dreamed of having a proper Swiss watch.

John and Kerim fished unsuccessfully in the Temnik this evening. Nik and John are hoping to wake up early to catch some breakfast. They should arise to a beautiful sight for the night is crystal clear and this valley is an alpine gem of storybook quality.

The night is clear and cold and I am looking forward to sleeping under the stars.

Overleaf:
Left: Buryat children outside a shop
(J.B.)

Right: Buryat girl
(J.B.)

24TH JUNE, IN THE TAIGA OF THE HAMAR DABAN MOUNTAINS, SOUTH OF BABUSHKIN

Hamar Daban means Big Mountains in Buryat. We are at their eastern end, near where they meet the Selenge River. Today's ride of about twenty miles took us through dense forest rising steeply along both sides of the logging road along which we rode. Logging is very clearly the primary, if not the only, form of human land use in this region.

Environmental laws at the Russian Federation level forbid almost all logging in the watershed of Lake Baikal. This much we knew before coming here. From Piotr, we try to ascertain the details of loopholes, enforcement and local legislation. Back at home it was impossible to get accurate information on Russian forestry regulations and it doesn't seem much easier here. He says that to cut a tree legally within the watershed, you must receive permission from the regional authority, in this case the Buryat Republic, and also from the Russian Federation. The logging that we have witnessed is probably being done at the behest of the municipal authorities of Ozero Goustnoye, Goose Lake, the nearest town.

The background is predictable. Piotr says that the Buryat Republic and its local authorities allow logging within the watershed unofficially and then pretend that the logs were cut outside the watershed, enabling them to collect taxes on the transactions and bribes from the parties involved. The corruption reaches all the way to Moscow, say Genia and Piotr, where officials at the Ministry of Forestry earn 'big money' for turning a blind eye. If the cover is blown, a scapegoat is chosen, paid to take the heat, and shifted to another job.

The workers are wildcatters from all over Russia, men who come out here to work for a few years. As poverty, lawlessness and despair set in after the collapse of the USSR, the frontier lands and their natural riches attract society's marginal players – the hardest cases and those with least to lose. The Old West, contemporary Amazonia, Siberia since its discovery and so on: it is an old story.

Genia hates the loggers. He says that most of them are from west of the Urals, from European Russia.

'Their homeland is far away from here,' he says. 'They have a saying: "If it jumps more than five centimetres, shoot it."'

Piotr says, 'It is not the fault of the loggers. It is the men in charge whom we must blame.'

Once we had left the Buryat steppe behind us and entered the taiga, it became clear that the logging south of Baikal was far more intense than that in Mongolia. Entire hillsides were scarred with clear-cuts. Logging roads had eroded long stretches of river banks, despoiling in many places the flat, gravelly beds that are crucial breeding grounds for several of the trout and other salmonid species so important to the aquatic food chain in Baikal and its watershed.

The cutting, ultimately financed by Japanese, Taiwanese and Korean corporations, was said to be paid for with Russian cars assembled far to the west. So many cubic metres of wood got you a Lada, more got you a Volga, and so on. But how much wood was being cut? What were the authorities really doing? Hard information was depressingly hard to find, then and later. The workers in the logging operations refused to speak to us, other than to convey threats or curses, and the claims of our companions could not be assumed to be scrupulously accurate. Russians are infamously predisposed to conspiracy theories of the paranoid, and usually xenophobic, type and we soon learned to believe the gist of what we were told, but not the details.

Meanwhile the push to Baikal was going smoothly. Taran's hand was bloated to nearly half-again its normal size for several days after being bitten by a spider, and the thumb-half of my right hand was numb for the next few weeks, presumably for the same reason. Sergei had sores on his calves from the stirrup leathers of his Russian saddle and Nik had some sort of stomach bug, but in general we were healthy.

Piotr was fitting in decently. His demeanour was irritatingly active and interfering, somewhat like that of a monkey, but he was useful around the camp and spoke with assurance on ecological topics.

The horses had taken well to our saddles and seemed to be a solid little crew. As the days passed, their various characters began to emerge. Back in Camp Selenge John and Nik had put their Mongolian experience to good use, choosing their new horses well. John had surprisingly gone for a small chestnut stallion called Dagaouz, soon changed to 'Digger', whose big ribs betrayed that he was older than the rest. Despite his size and age, Digger rewarded John's eye by being our joint-fastest horse at both a canter and a gallop. Nik had chosen Rizhka, Red, our second biggest horse and one who at first suffered from a truculent nature. Nik soon learned to cut a stout switch every morning and after a few days of bucking he had a strong and steady mount who was easily in our top rank over a quarter- to a half-mile. I was encouraged to see that it was Genia who had made the best pick of all, a pick that it took a subtle eye to make. His horse was called Tofka, Russian for 'Tough Guy', and he was a little Yakut pony with a cheery disposition and a heart like a lion when the trail was tricky. He was a lightning bolt out of the blocks and, although over a distance Digger could usually catch him, Tough Guy was never actually beaten.

Sergei was doing well with a reliable, if uninspiring, gelding also called Rizhka. As for Sergei's two fellow newcomers to the equine world, Taran learned that Siberia is no place for aesthetes when Malish, a bay gelding with a slender, elegant build and a dashing white blaze on his forehead, turned out to be the dog of the lot, slow, dull and stupid. Kerim soon became equally disappointed with his mount.

A black gelding with white socks, Karka was our oldest horse. He was also our biggest but the excitement of this soon wore off for poor Kerim when the old boy revealed that he would not canter, could not

gallop, and limped when he trotted.

Our goal as we rode north through southern Buryatia was a town called Babushkin, a fishing and forestry community of a thousand hardy souls perched at the eastern end of the lake's south coast. At Babushkin we would turn west and follow Baikal's shore in a three-month clockwise circuit that would, we hoped, land us back in Babushkin before the autumn storms made the coastline impassable and the snows came and the rivers started to freeze. Once they did freeze, in late October, they would change from obstacles to welcome stretches of flat footing. But on either end of the big freeze is the little freeze, when you and your horse can get into the water easily enough but you can't get out.

Opposite:
Logging road through the taiga
(K.Y.)

9:20 A.M., 26TH JUNE, THE EAST BANK OF THE MISOVKA RIVER, FOUR MILES SOUTH OF BABUSHKIN
Today, we shall see Lake Baikal for the first time. We aim to mount up at ten this morning and reach Babushkin at eleven thirty. We have all slept well. Nikolai has recovered from a stomach illness, the horses are healthy, and it is a breezy sunny morning. We are about to eat well of hard-boiled eggs and baked beans. Baikal is only four miles away – so close that Genia says he can smell it.

1 Forsyth, J.A. (1992) *A History of the Peoples of Siberia: Russia's North Asian Colony*, Cambridge.
2 Ibid.

chapter five

BAIKAL'S SOUTH COAST

AFTER two years of planning and dreaming, after five hundred miles in the saddle, we were at last about to see the waters of the world's largest lake. Holy to many, twenty-five million years old, as beautiful and important and mysterious as any place on earth, Lake Baikal beckoned us on that June morning with all the promise of a hundred Xs on a hundred pirate treasure maps.

Opposite:
Logging on the shores
of Lake Baikal
(K.Y.)

Most of us ate slowly around the breakfast fire but John gulped down his food and dashed off into the taiga and out of sight. Such behaviour usually signified intestinal crisis, but not this time. John soon re-emerged into our small clearing carrying a thin, five-foot length of birch cut from a sapling in a nearby stand. 'Today', he announced, 'we ride with the flag'. He stripped the sapling of its bark, cut a couple of notches near the narrow end, and tied on our expedition flag with its gold Mongol warrior on a field of Central Asian red and the Sacred Sea blue against a taiga green. Twenty minutes later we were saddled up and ready to go.

On the outskirts of Babushkin, with a low line of hills delaying our first view of Lake Baikal, we stopped at the headquarters of the Babushkin Forestry Office. There were two equipment sheds, an outhouse and a little office building, all wooden and threadbare. Piotr passed his first test well by persuading the Director to meet us for an hour.

Under the ultimate jurisdiction of the Russian Federation Ministry of Forestry, the Forestry Office was responsible for protecting the taiga of the Babushkin District from pestilence, forest fires and illegal logging. The Director and his three rangers were looking after more than a thousand square miles of thick and largely untracked taiga. Until 1990, he said, they'd been quite well funded. After perestroika, however, money was the main problem.

'Life is difficult,' the Director said. 'My rangers are paid almost nothing, thirty dollars a month. They are like beggars. How much can I ask of them?'

This sentiment was to recur often as we rode around Lake Baikal. The radical upheavals of Gorbachev's perestroika were being blamed for the poverty of the Russian state. And before perestroika, said the Director, glasnost had lifted the oppressive sense that all of life was dictated by the state.

'Now people feel free,' he said. 'They think glasnost and perestroika mean that they can do whatever they want. It's as if everything is allowed.' For Russia's forest rangers, just as for its cellists, scientists and weight-lifters, life had been easier in the bad old days.

Few of the ecological problems in the Director's region had much effect on the health of Lake Baikal, he said. Forest fires sometimes damaged the sources of minor tributaries, but the fires were usually caused by lightning. The logging in his area was minimal, about 11,000 cubic metres annually, maybe fifty big lorry-loads. Most of this was what is called 'sanitary' logging, the profitable extraction of dead or dying trees without which the current and rising generations of trees, especially those of selected species such as cedar, should theoretically grow more freely.

In other cases the purpose of the logging was to clear routes for power lines or roads. This was more disturbing. Route-logging encouraged the choice of routes where the logging would be most profitable. The Director told us that he was trying to fine the builders of a new power line. They had failed to clean up after themselves and they also had to pay for the cedar they had taken out.

The Director's domain did appear to be far better managed than Gousino-Ozersk, the last forestry district through which we had ridden. There we had seen lorry after lorry bearing illegal cedar cuttings. One would be naive not to expect a ranger who has discovered illegal logging to forego the fine and split the difference with the loggers. Salaries of $30 a month, the erosion of the state, and the decay of confidence in collective values do not encourage rigorous stewardship of the land. Was the Director impressed with the principles of his peers elsewhere in Buryatia?

'Good question,' he said. 'Those who cut cedar take advantage of Russia's current situation. But I'd rather not talk too honestly about them. I'm sorry I have to be so diplomatic...'

As he had expressed a degree of personal sympathy with our project, I invited him to meet us on Baikal's shore for lunch. His eyes lit up.

'It has been a long time since I have ridden a horse,' he said with a big smile. 'Perhaps you could lend me one and give me the pleasure of leading you down to the lake?'

We put him on our sunny little friend Tofka and they led us down the dusty streets winding between Babushkin's bare wooden houses and picket-fenced kitchen gardens. We rode through a petrol station, across a marshy hollow, up the steep stone bank of the Trans-Siberian, across the train-tracks and down the other side. After a stand of birch trees we emerged onto a flat shelf of grassland atop a twenty-foot cliff with a rocky beach at its foot.

And there in all its vast majesty was the lake of lakes. To left and right, north-east and south-west, the horizon was water. Straight ahead, forty miles away, were the Primorskiy Mountains of the southern West Coast. An onshore breeze, cooled by waters that had been ice a few weeks earlier, blew primeval life at us over the blue depths.

Lunch of salted omul and a
bottle of Moldovan red
(K.Y.)

Overleaf:
Baikal by night
(J.B.)

In the shade of a lone, stunted tree we washed down bread, salted fish
and tinned beef with a litre of vodka and two bottles of sturdy Moldovan
red wine. The fish was omul, a delicious cousin of the salmon and one
of Lake Baikal's thirty unique species of fish. The salty taste and smooth
red flesh of the omul, caught that morning, somehow made our cheap
vodka feel smooth as velvet.

6:30 P.M., 26TH JUNE, OUTSIDE OF BABUSHKIN, ON THE SOUTH COAST OF LAKE BAIKAL
Baikal is larger and somehow even grander than we had expected. The West Coast is only forty
miles away and we can see it easily on this sunny afternoon. The water churns against the shore
in eight-inch swells. Small settlements and structures dot this shore to north and south of us.
Somehow, the relatively prosaic scale of these details notwithstanding, Baikal has a sense of
majesty, of latent power, that we all feel but can't quite explain. The lake is a curiously potent
enigma. Perhaps the explanation is connected to its deceptiveness: we can see the other side, the
waves are small, and the hand of man has touched its shores, and yet despite all of this Baikal
explodes into death-dealing storms and earthquakes, holds secrets that science hasn't fathomed
and lives an intricate and unique life of its own that man has not yet been able to derange.

I looked up from my journal and saw that the setting sun had turned the
lake into a great basin of molten gold. What was this miracle that I was
looking at?

Two things make Lake Baikal important. First, it is the earth's single
biggest reservoir of fresh water. It contains 20 per cent of the liquid
fresh water on this planet. If Baikal's 23,000 cubic kilometres of water
were strung together in 1-kilometre cubes, they would reach from the
north pole to the south pole and 3,000 kilometres beyond. In human
terms this means that if the whole world started using water at the

65

highest current urban consumption rates, Lake Baikal could supply our needs for fifty years.

The second reason why Lake Baikal is so important is science. It is, as *The New Scientist* has said, 'the most fascinating freshwater ecosystem on earth'. Even an abbreviated list of its superlatives can be numbing. Of all the world's lakes, Lake Baikal is the deepest, largest, oldest, coldest and cleanest. In it are the only freshwater seals and the only freshwater thermal vents in the world. It lies in the deepest terrestrial rift on earth. Among water ecosystems it is unrivalled for the sheer number of its species; among ecosystems generally, it has the highest rate of endemism, for over three-quarters of its species exist nowhere else.

When we started planning our expedition, in 1991, scientists estimated that Baikal was home to twelve hundred unique species of flora and fauna. When we departed for Mongolia in May of 1993, the consensus had reached thirteen hundred. As Kerim and I sat on that clifftop after our first lunch by Baikal's waters, we laughed about 'species inflation' and wondered where it might stop. By 1997, the estimates were at fifteen hundred and counting.

What are all these species? They include plankton, molluscs, crustaceans, sponges and fish. At the top of the food chain is the nerpa, *Phoca sibirica*, the only seal in the world that lives in fresh water. As is the case with many of Lake Baikal's natural phenomena, scientists disagree about the nerpa's origins. The main debate is about whether they came from the Caspian Sea or the Arctic. Hunters, most of them Buryats, are allowed to kill about 10 per cent of the lake's sixty thousand nerpa every winter. Somehow I felt better about these furry creatures bleating out their death cries on the ice when I learned that the nerpa themselves are unusually greedy predators. Each one eats about two tons of fish and plankton annually.

Among the lake's thirty unique species of fish is a bizarre creature called the golomyanka. Alone among the fish of the northern hemisphere, the golomyanka is viviparous, which means that it gives birth to live young. Some scientists say it eats its young, others say it can't possibly do so because it dies immediately after releasing its two thousand live offspring. If it does eat its young it certainly doesn't eat all of them, for at any given time there are about five billion golomyanka living in Baikal, weighing a total of 165,000 tons. In terms of weight this is the equivalent of almost fifty thousand adult great white sharks. The most astounding thing about the golomyanka is that it lives at every water level down to 1,500 metres, and manages to do so without an air bladder to help it handle the changes in pressure. This is more impressive than it might sound. Mark Sergeyev, a well-known Siberian author, tells of a scientific researcher who, trying to obtain a water sample from Baikal's middle depths, dropped a steel chamber to 500 metres but forgot to open its pressure valve. When the chamber was hauled to the surface it had been 'crushed by the water as if it had been made of tinfoil and not of steel'. [1]

Scientists do not know how the golomyanka manages what reinforced submarines can't, but they do know that at about 1,300 metres of depth, when the water is exerting a force of over 1,900 pounds per square inch, the density of the golomyanka's tissue changes by some mysterious physiological process. Because the golomyanka are small and don't swim in schools, they can be hard to catch and harder to study. If you bring them to the surface too quickly they can explode and if you leave them somewhere warm they will melt, for half their bodyweight is fat. As a result of the latter characteristic they are translucent, which has given rise to the local bromide that you could read a newspaper through one if you wanted to.

Lake Baikal's unparalleled degree of endemism is the result of its extraordinary physical characteristics. Coldness, age, size, depth, purity and isolation from other openwater ecosystems – in each of these regards Baikal is unique. If the lake possessed only one of these attributes it would be a special place. Because it possesses all of them, in ecosystem terms it is almost Another Planet. It is therefore a resource of unsurpassed importance for the scientific nexus where biology, evolution and the geographical disciplines meet.

The key concept is the evolution of unique species in unique surroundings. Some of the lake's endemic species are what biologists call relics – they are survivors from eons past. Many of the lake's molluscs and sponges, for example, pre-date the seismic activity that created the rift zone in which Baikal lies. Others among Baikal's endemic species – whole families and interlocking systems of them, not just isolated mutations perpetuated by quirks of geography – evolved within the lake during its twenty-five million years. Almost all of these endemic species live in Baikal's open waters, in the so-called 'pillagel' zone, where, unlike in the coastal zones, they are utterly dominant. In the pillagel, which remains uncontaminated by pollution, the endemic ecosystem continues to function in its natural ways. This is where Baikal teaches its most precious lessons to scientists. And this is why, apart from its status as the world's reservoir, Baikal is worth protecting.

Historians believe that Genghis Khan was born near Baikal's South Coast, probably in 1167. His birthplace was by the Onon River, a tributary of the Selenge. Since long before then, since Paleolithic times, man and Baikal have coexisted. Until 1959 that coexistence was perfectly harmonious. In that year, Moscow determined to build a factory to produce wood-based cellulose at a South Coast village called Baikalsk. Super-clean water was needed for the production of high-grade wood pulp to be used in tire cords for the new bombers and military transport aircraft being developed at that time, the heyday of the Cold War.

In an era when dissent was dangerous and the defence establishment nearly omnipotent in the Soviet Union, the Russian environmental movement was born, like the Great Khan, near Baikal's southern shore. Centred around a core of brave souls based at the Irkutsk office of the Siberian Branch of the Soviet Academy of Sciences, scientists, intellectuals, artists and religious figures from across the Soviet Union took serious personal risks to protest against the defilement of Lake Baikal, which was, and is, Russia's most beloved natural treasure. But their first efforts were doomed. The building of the Baikalsk pulp mill went ahead and it was followed by a second big factory, the Selenginsk Pulp and Carton Plant. The central-planners erected a new town at the northern tip of the West Coast. The Angara River, Baikal's sole effluent, was dammed; this raised the lake's water level by up to a metre, enough to change coastal erosion patterns and disrupt the reproduction of omul, trout and other fish that spawn in shallow water.

But the early efforts of the Russian environmental movement were not entirely in vain. Consciousness of Baikal's importance has been raised, so that the Russian public knows and cares about the lake's ecological problems. State policy has been influenced. When the second pulp mill was built, at Selenginsk near the mouth of the Selenge River, a closed-cycle filtration system was developed so that, theoretically, the waste water is cleaned and then reused. The new town, Severo-Baikalsk, was also designed with waste-treatment as an ostensible priority. It is now considered highly unlikely that further factories or new towns will be built in the lake's immediate vicinity.

On our first day on Lake Baikal we rode about seventeen miles, at first along pretty paths by the lake and then along the two-lane coastal road to the tune of honking truck drivers and groaning Ladas. It was only the second time we had ridden on tarmac roads. The first time had been the previous day, when the flag we carried on John's birch pole elicited a far more positive response from drivers than we received without it. We took their surliness for granted.

That night we camped in a pretty green and yellow meadow, and before supper we had our first swim in the holy waters. Baikal was very cold, as cold as we had expected. The South Coast is considered to be the industrialised, overpopulated arm-pit of Baikal, but the water was extremely clear. Nonetheless, said the local rangers, even there it was polluted by the Baikalsk pulp mill. We struggled to imagine the wildness and beauty of the northern two-thirds of Baikal's shoreline, where the water was still said to be utterly pristine. In the lake's offshore pillagel zone, here in the south as much as in the wild north, the phyto-plankton, sponges, amphipods, molluscs and vertical circulation currents were busy making the purest water anywhere.

Housed in a low-ceilinged log cabin, our first Russian sauna – the famous *banya* – was a delight. After our swim, Piotr spent an hour choosing bits of split logs and jamming them into the banya's rough-soldered iron furnace, a rusty box with special rocks piled on top and a pipe leading the smoke out through the roof. He moved more quickly and muttered more loudly as the temperature rose. When the banya was ready we took turns going in to learn the ritual from this wide-eyed zealot. Slimy hand-cut wooden benches lined the walls of the banya and large tin bowls full of water were laid out upon the floor. After steaming for about twenty minutes, you soaped up, rinsed yourself with a bucket of hot water, flagellated yourself with birch branches, and then emerged dazed and gasping into the sunlight for a final cold rinse.

We were tingling and fresh for supper and celebrated our first swim in the Sacred Sea with some Moldovan red and a bottle of vodka. The Baikalsk Nature Preserve ranger whose compound we were sharing for the night was a tall, dark, burly man who looked as if he knew how to handle the rivers and snow-storms and grizzlies that are his lot. His monthly salary added up to about a dollar a day and his team had nothing but a broken motorcycle for transport.

Kerim asked him why he stuck with the job.

'All my life I wanted to live in the taiga,' the ranger said. 'I grew up in a city, Samara. It is in the south of European Russia and all around me was farmland and steppe. I loved those open spaces but, deep inside, every Russian wants to be in the taiga.' He moved out to Baikal at the age of twenty, as soon as he had finished his military service.

The next morning we started a five-hour slog along the newly cut path of the Buryat-Energo power line. We had expected it to be a short-cut but we were wrong. It was a swath of devastation one hundred yards wide and many miles long, strewn with mutilated trees and somewhat like no-man's-land on the Somme. The horses were often stuck in the many marshy passages and the ooze belched and stank as they struggled free. We picked our way slowly through the pitfalls of rotting trees. 'Wait until we ride through the taiga itself. This will seem easy,' said Piotr.

At three thirty that afternoon we came back onto the two-lane tarmac road. After a quick lunch of boiled potatoes and tinned beans we set off once more down the long dreary asphalt, through a sunny afternoon,

Overleaf, left and right: Children in Tanhoy *(J.B.)*

hot at last; for the first time we rode with our shirts off. The cold of Mongolia seemed a long way off but even so we knew the Siberian summer would be short.

We passed through a village called Tanhoy. It was early evening, that magic time of the summer day when children are released from the supper table to charge about in the long evening light. Tanhoy's muddy main street buzzed with little boys and girls on tricycles and bicycles. Several of them, the braver ones, rode alongside us as we clip-clopped through town. As we learned to smile and wave we received many smiles and waves in return.

After three more days on the tarmac, a road sign and a huge smokestack looming up through the taiga announced that we were approaching Baikalsk, where the pulp mill is the lake's single worst polluter. The factory itself is run with a paranoid degree of secrecy and even before leaving the United States we had been warned that we would never be allowed a meeting with the management, much less a tour of the facility. And so it was.

Baikalsk is also home to the Institute of Ecological Toxicology, which studies pollution in Baikal. Piotr was an old friend of a Dr Pavlov, the Institute's Director, who agreed to meet us. After showing us his laboratories he took us to the artificial pond where the mill's waste is held until it is discharged directly into the lake through huge underwater pipes. Earlier he had told us that any trauma less powerful than five hundred-megaton bombs would not upset Lake Baikal's ecological balance. Baikal is so huge and its unique self-cleaning mechanisms of vertical water circulation and waste-eating plankton are so strong that he could well be close to the truth.

We joined him later for a drink and salted omul at his little clapboard house a couple of miles outside Baikalsk. He had just heard on the radio that President Yeltsin had cut the state scientific budget by 10 per cent and removed the inflation indexation. At the prevailing rates of inflation this meant that Pavlov's salary was likely to halve in real terms by the end of the year. His wife was the Director of the Biological Institute at Irkutsk University, a scientist as eminent and vulnerable as himself. Pavlov was a stooped man of about fifty-five long years, wheezing, ill-looking and weary. His stuttering kindness made the bad news rather tragic.

Among several other meetings on this South Coast leg of the expedition were two sessions at the headquarters of the Baikalskoye Biosphere Preserve. The unlit two-storey building was picturesque in its boxy grey bleakness. A Women's Association bulletin board hung empty in a corridor, and stencilled Communist iconography flaked from the walls. Our first meeting was with the Assistant Director for Ecological

Education, one of the Preserve's resident research scientists, and a female botanist working on the Siberian edition of the *Green Book*, the UN-sponsored global catalogue of endangered species. They had the look of professional ecologists and field scientists the world over, as if they'd taken their cue from the marine biologist in *Jaws*. They were passionate about Baikal and in their eyes was that energetic, hopeful pathos of small-time crusaders. Only optimists could fight their fight so diligently, but the constant losing cuts a pessimistic facet onto those bright convictions. We spoke to them in the exhibit room of the Preserve offices, surrounded by glass cases housing mounted butterflies, fungi, barks and leaves. Stuffed musk deer, lynx, bear, owl, otters and other fauna lined the walls in a variety of awkward poses.

The Baikalskoye Biosphere Preserve encompassed over 412,000 acres of wild and varied terrain, reaching southward from Baikal's South Coast deep into the mountains of the Hamar Daban. The Preserve's plateaus, high mountain ridges, alpine meadows, coastline and taiga are home to over eight hundred species of flora, of which forty were then endangered.

We were given a poignant introduction to all of this through a screening of a short film which one of the scientists had made four years previously. Called *Next to You*, it was a clumsy, shaky effort that seemed to ache with the difficulty of its making and preservation, almost screaming out an unintended message about the frustration and talent of the Russian intelligentsia. We watched the original reel, which they treated like gold, as no money had ever been available for a copy. It had travelled all the way to and back from Italy's Fifth International Festival of Documentary Films on Parks. Blurred from too many viewings, played against the hum and rattle of an aged projector, shot on 1960s film that gave a dated, chromatic look to the images of salmon, wildflowers and snowy mountain vistas, the film seemed to summarise the demise of the state system that had once looked after its scientists and rangers so well even as it ravaged its natural treasures. As the Preserve included neither towns nor industrial enterprises and was almost entirely composed of healthy wilderness, little that happened inside it ranked among the major threats to Baikal. Nonetheless there were many problems in the Preserve that related directly to the health of the lake.

'Our area', said the Assistant Director, 'contributes unique aspects of Baikal's biodiversity. One of our trees, the blue fir, is a good example. This species is unique in the whole world, but they cut the new power line right through its most important habitat.

'It is bad enough when Chinese workers are imported, but they work neatly. The Russian loggers just cut all the trees, take away the convenient ones, leave the others to rot. So you can see for yourselves the attitude that we are fighting. The Babushkin Forestry Office filed a complaint in court against Buryat-Energo but they were told to consider the energy needs of the country and not to make a big scandal.

'In terms of atmospheric pollution', said the woman, 'this is the most sensitive part of Baikal, but we have no money to study it. The prevailing wind currents blow air pollution in this direction from regions far to the west. There are aluminium plants in Irkutsk and Bratsk. There are chemical plants at Krasnoyarsk and along the Angara River. They pump chemicals into the atmosphere and the Hamar Daban Mountains form a natural pipeline that dumps it all in this part of Baikal. Tanhoy means Rotten Corner in Buryat, because so much rain falls here. In the mountains we have 1,500 millimetres of rain a year as opposed to 800 on the coast.

'This rain is polluted and our trees are suffering. The coniferous trees, which should purify the water entering Baikal, are like a pollution barometer. They are smaller than they used to be, their reproductive cycles are longer. In the mountains you can see that the needles of the more sensitive species are often brown or yellow, not green.

'We have no laboratory here, no money to make precise measurements of this pollution. But our science department has been collecting water samples since 1986. They send the samples to the Institute of Ecological Toxicology and also to the Limnological Institute in Irkutsk. But official access to this data is expensive. We try to get access through personal contacts...'

The worst threat to Baikal, they said, was the industrial plants – especially the pulp mills. Local people were becoming increasingly concerned about the ecological problems and apparently there were some good programmes in a few of the schools. As the Assistant Director said, 'People fear for their own health.'

They were critical of most of the West's attempts to help. 'There is big money involved with Baikal, but it doesn't come to places like this. It goes to the institutes in Irkutsk and Ulan Ude, where they create a tourist industry for foreign scientists rather than conduct real ecological research. Much of the money goes to administration. The institutes get video equipment and holiday cottages. The Preserves don't even have their own laboratories.

'You should send the money to the people who work with it directly. If it goes to some institute in a big city the people on the ground will never see the results, whereas we will buy equipment directly and use it directly.' It was with solid feelings of encouragement that we said good-bye and went upstairs to await our interview with their boss, the Director of the Preserve. Upon seeing the Director, Nikolai suggested to me that I start the interview by apologising for waking him. A

Communist-era appointee from Ulan Ude, a classic old-time apparatchik, he was more on his toes than he looked. He had a good opportunity to show off his Soviet stuff when confronted with this bunch of starry-eyed, pesky foreign enthusiasts.

It soon became obvious that his chosen technique for satisfying interview requests while giving nothing away was simply to talk as much as possible on ground of his own choosing until the allotted time was over. About four times in half an hour, I was able to seize a pause at the end of Sergei's translation and pose a question to the Director.

Opposite:
Buryat fisherman,
circa 1948

He would respond obliquely and then wander off on further pre-emptive tangents, all the while staring at his paperless desk or out of the window. He never stopped playing with his spectacles, an activity that belied his calm, bureaucratic voice.

'What is the single most effective thing that can be done to protect Lake Baikal?' I asked.

'You, the young people, should know better than I. Understanding between peoples and the commitment of the youth are the two most important things for Baikal,' he said.

It was obvious that the meeting would render little value or sense. It was extremely sad. The three people we had met in the first meeting were straight, self-sacrificing, idealistic souls. It was a horror to think of their energy being constantly dashed on the granite cliff of a system full of Directors.

We rode from two o'clock that afternoon until almost ten at night and camped in a pretty spot on the verge of a field on Baikal's shore. On the way, we counted eighty-six four-wheel vehicles, seventy-one six-and-more-wheelers, seven motorbikes with side-cars, four solo motorbikes, and four trains clattering down the old tracks of the Trans-Siberian railway. Things were getting much busier as we neared Irkutsk.

Our ultimate destination as we rode west along the South Coast was a small seismological station a few miles inland from Baikal's south-western corner. The station lay in the deep taiga of the foothills rising up from the lake to the western end of the Hamar Daban Mountains. Our plan was to leave the horses at the station to rest while our supply truck took us to Irkutsk. Genia would stay with the seismologists and the horses and try to arrange for us to buy or rent a couple more of the latter.

On the last afternoon of that dreary week-long trek along the South Coast tarmac, we had the ride of our lives. With only ten miles between us and the seismic station, we waited for the day's heat to pass before we saddled-up. We set off in a sunny summer shower and rode on into a clear evening. After the rain the air was soft and smelled of ozone.

That evening's stretch of road was carved high into the flanks of the

mountains and we stopped three times to enjoy the views. Baikal was still new to us and it was exciting just to see its blue horizons. We passed above three pretty old villages on the narrow flats between the slopes and the train-tracks, which follow the shore. As we rounded the last high bend, we saw below us a town called Sludyanka. It was about eight thirty in the evening and the light was rosy and gentle. Baikal was perfectly calm, its flatness relieved only by a few fishermen sitting still and solitary in their wooden row-boats. The boats were of a design peculiar to Lake Baikal. They were simple, mastless and rudderless, nothing but a plain curve of gunwale rising to a sharp undercut stern and a sharper bow. The sight made me think of one of Russia's great folk-songs, 'Thoughts of a Fugitive on Baikal'. Months later I found a full translation:

Sacred Baikal – glorious sea,
An old omul barrel – my glorious ship.
Ho, North Wind, stir the waves for me,
And hasten a brave lad's trip.

Heavy chains I dragged for many a day,
Through the hills of Akatui I went.
An old friend helped me run away,
I came to life with freedom's scent.

Shilka, Nerchinsk, I've been everywhere,
The mountain police didn't catch me,
In the forest the gluttonous beast kept his lair,
No rifleman's bullet could scratch me.

By dark and broad daylight I fled,
Near the towns I glanced left and right,
The peasant women would give me bread,
The lads kept my pipe alight.

Sacred Baikal – glorious sea,
A kaftan in holes – my glorious sail.
Ho, North Wind, stir the waves for me,
Peals of thunder portend a gale.[2]

In contrast to the green coast and pink-tinged blue sky and water bordering it, Sludyanka presented a dirty grey face as we first saw it from the road above. Say Sludyanka ten times and you start to think that somewhere in the distance are a thousand wretched souls shovelling coal and a hundred iron behemoths clashing their dinosaur limbs. Industrial and sooty, it lived up to its name. Riding through the town took about twenty minutes. Along the way a couple of hundred of the inhabitants

Left:
19th-century
Siberian convicts:
Dreaming of an
'old omul barrel' and an
escape to freedom
across Baikal?

Overleaf:
Left:
Babushka, Sludyanka
(J.B.)

Right:
Two boys fishing,
Sludyanka
(K.Y.)

stopped their work in gardens and markets and garages to watch us pass. We had ridden through small towns, but never such a big settlement at that time of day and never with our flag flying. There were children riding along beside us on their bicycles and clusters of people cheered us on from several streets away. At an empty lot where about forty children and teenagers had gathered, we stopped to enjoy our fame. One girl insisted on being photographed with Taran, and I lent her Sarge for the shot. Another girl was keen to practise her English. After five minutes two policemen drove up in a peeling Lada and told us it was time to move on.

We set off at a discreet trot which soon degenerated into a mighty clattering canter through the streets, with the flag fluttering at the head of the line and Genia leading us in, bellowing loudly. His exuberance was always palpably infectious among horses and men alike. There's never been a grin like the one on Genia's face during a long canter. In Sludyanka he developed what was to be his war-cry for the next thousand miles. 'Hellooo cheeldren!' he roared out as we passed little gaggles of kids. With his round face flushed and his eyes wide open with excitement he was like a Siberian Father Christmas with a Yakut pony for a sled.

At nine o'clock we turned off that South Coast tarmac for the last time and followed a dirt road through several large potato fields and up into the taiga. It had been a short ride and the horses were still fresh. We charged on in a new series of canters and gallops, winding through the twilit forest up and up into the hills. To those so inclined, it is the stuff of dreams to career through the woods in the long shadows of a warm summer evening, flag in hand, roaring out like Pancho Villa after a quart of tequila, with your best friends in full cry around you. We slowed for a breather a couple of times and once saw a couple of boys hiding behind a fence in the woods, watching us.

1 Sergeyev, M. (1989) *The Wonders and Problems of Lake Baikal*, Moscow.
2 Tupper, H. (1965) *To the Great Ocean: Siberia and the Trans-Siberian Railway*, Boston.
    Song translated by M.S. Shatz.

81

chapter six

IRKUTSK, PARIS OF SIBERIA

O N the 2nd of July, after two nights in the seismological station, we left Genia with the horses, piled into our re-supply lorry and set off for Irkutsk, the chief city of Eastern Siberia and the Baikal region. While the horses rested and ate, Genia would shoe those that needed it and try to procure a couple more from a nearby collective farm.

As we rattled down the sixty-mile tarmac leading to Irkutsk, dozing off on piles of saddle blankets and burlap sacks of oats, it seemed a far better way to travel than clopping along on horseback. Half an hour later, Taran passed me a bag of tobacco and some papers and said, 'This is no way to travel. Look at us, slumped around, lying down. Staring at the floor. What have we seen in the last half an hour?' The answer was easy. Nothing.

Riding a horse through steppe and taiga can be monotonous, but there is no better way to see the country. The walker stares at the heels of the man in front. The motorist is stultified by the engine's throb and the speed of the scenery flashing past. The rider on horseback has both a need for vigilance and the opportunity for contemplation. This sensitivity to the details of the landscape gives meaning to the broader views and an intimacy with the character of the land. The rider sees over the country with eyes half human and half animal. He thinks of footing, pasture, water, but his mind, sparked and resparked all day by the need to be alert, often reaches out over the horizon.

My reverie ended when Piotr shouted out to stop the vehicle. Winking at us with his wide, crooked grin, he grabbed an axe, leaped from the lorry, and plunged into the taiga. He stopped ten feet into the bush and began to cut small green branches off young birch trees, severing them neatly at the joints with his axe. With each stroke a little pixie of a ring hovered in the taiga before dying away. Piotr was a maestro with an axe, quick and sure of his aim. This particular axe, his favourite, had a head of steel so pure and hard it held vibrations like a tuning fork. After two minutes he emerged with a huge armload of the leafy branches. '*Banya!*' he cried. Of course: bath-house flagellation branches, the local equivalent of the loofah sponges favoured by Californians between encounter groups and of the lead scrapers that befuddled Imperial Rome.

Lunch awaited us at Piotr's house on the far side of town. The house was a *dacha*, a small country cottage which, like so many Russians, he used to escape the city and to grow vegetables for the winter. Piotr's *dacha* was a single-storey building with five decently spacious rooms. It and its thirty-or-so neighbours were separated from each other by wooden stockades and muddy dirt streets. Twenty yards from Piotr's, a

Opposite:
'Denouncing a Dastard' –
poster for an 1890s
Broadway play

small stream widened briefly into a flat, gravelly pool where half a dozen children played and swam. Like every other residence we had seen in Russia and Mongolia, the *dacha* was shabby and quite clean. Inside, paint flaked from the walls and ceilings and the rooms were dotted with cheap, generally pink decorations of the doily type. A large cast-iron stove squatted like an ogre-king in the sparsely furnished kitchen.

Piotr's wife, Marina, was a thin, cheery woman who seemed to relish the opportunity to mother us all. She gave us dumpling soup, sausages and a good tomato and cucumber salad, which we ate with a bottle of Spanish white wine and some vodka. Afterwards, John, Nikolai and Kerim fell asleep on a sofa by the table. Taran moved to the other end of the room with a local newspaper and sank down into a big chair. I joined him and it was bliss, for although we couldn't read Russian the rough age-yellowed newsprint, the oily feel of the ink and the sound of turning pages were all we needed. A quarter of an hour later, Piotr, drunk again in his hyperactive, gibbering way, decided that I wanted a nap and manhandled me into a bedroom.

After a slow count to a hundred, I sneaked out of my little guestroom prison and past the already creaking mattress springs of Piotr's bedroom. Nik had awoken and the two of us took our sleeping bag pads out into the yard for a nap in the sun. Strewn with wood chips, old buckets and the droppings of the dog and pigs that wandered freely in and out, the courtyard was a dirt and cement enclosure between the house and a three-sided wooden stockade fence.

We were woken an hour later by Piotr chopping wood in a drunken frenzy a few paces away. He paused every minute or two to rush to his little *banya* and stoke the furnace. The old maniacal leer was back on his craggy face. He was like a Rider Haggard priest preparing for some bloody rite, somewhere between possession and rapture in the service of a God who liked his offerings burnt. Nikolai and I watched in terror as Piotr split the logs ever thinner, muttering slackly to himself as he held a splinter of wood upright on the chopping block with the forefinger of his left hand while with the right he brought that favourite axe swinging down.

The furnace was soon well-stoked and there was no denying our host as he prodded and jabbered us out of our comfortable slumbers. Including laundry and several breaks for fresh air, Piotr's *banya* turned into a three-hour extravaganza. He would throw more water on the stove and then more as we gasped for air and crouched low to avoid the steam. Unannounced and unsolicited, he started beating Nikolai with the faggot of birch branches gathered on the way to Irkutsk. Naked, beet-red and sweating, shouting and thrashing about hunched low

Opposite:
Above:
Drunk and his lorry
(J.B.)

Below:
Nikolai and the author at
Piotr's *dacha*
(K.Y.)

87

under the roof-beams, Piotr was not a sight for the weak of heart.

At supper that night I tasted fresh beef for the first time in over a month. After endless mutton, tinned meat and salted fish, the bloody vitality was a revelation. The beef was well accompanied by three bottles of vodka and followed by two Russian songs and a round of Tamerlane Blues. Piotr's wife and son, Max, seemed perfectly comfortable with his drunkenness. We had noticed in a few of the South Coast towns how little concern people showed with regard to the ubiquitous drunks. They were treated like people with colds: you wouldn't really want to kiss them but there was nothing remarkable in their condition – no real response other than a hint of sympathy. Unless the drunks were Buryats, sober Siberians – wives, shopkeepers, village passers-by – seemed to look on them as though 'Aleksander Nikolayevich is blind drunk and being sick on his dog' was a remark about as worth making as 'Aleksander Nikolayevich is having a bad hair day.'

We spent the day reconnoitring the food shops for a big reprovisioning, trying to fix Taran's video microphone and scouting venues for the following night's Fourth of July dinner. The Soviet dreariness of the Intourist Hotel had a certain archaeological charm but that only went so far and the prices were steep. Through the windows of a pretty neoclassical building that bore the only good coat of paint in Irkutsk, we saw a lavish banquet laid out for that evening. I wondered how the Cossacks and fur-trappers of old Irkutsk must have felt when they saw the glittering society so often remarked upon by nineteenth-century visitors to the city. Ultimately we chose The Dragon, a small cheap Chinese restaurant.

Before heading back to Piotr's dacha, we had a beer in the Intourist Hotel's Genghis Khan Bar. In his day, the Great Khan used to retreat to the shores of Lake Baikal for thought, peace, and communion with the lake's mystical powers. He loved Baikal and after a day in the city I knew how the old boy felt. I couldn't wait to get back.

We arrived back at Piotr's dacha to find Genia awaiting us with his huge earthy grin and twinkling fur-trapper's eyes. It was wonderful to see that good face again, as if the taiga, the world of honesty and grit, was not so far away as a day in town had made it feel. It was still light after dinner, and Kerim, Taran, John, Nik and I read, talked and wrote, on the grass outside the dacha. Ten local kids milled about us as John and Max took turns playing Max's guitar. An old man from three houses down brought out an accordion and a bescarved *babushka* and two little girls danced a *troika*.

The next day, the Fourth of July, we met Dr Olga Kazhova, the wife of our friend Dr Pavlov. We spoke to Dr Kazhova for about an hour around the dining room table of their big flat. On the wall behind me hung an oil portrait of her father, the famous Dr Kazhov, wearing oilskins and a sou'wester and glaring into the teeth of a Baikal gale. He had been one of the giants of the previous generation of the lake's scientist adventurers.

A kindly and intelligent woman of sixty, Dr Kazhova showed a deep concern for Lake Baikal and a pessimistic view of its condition. Her assessment was radically different from that of her husband. Her voice trembled as she discussed Baikal's worst problems and several times the pain of it all seemed to bring her near to tears.

Kazhova was an eminent scientist in a field requiring high levels of precision. Nonetheless it was difficult to get from her a cogent argument that the long-term biological balance of the lake, and the factors which make it unique, are seriously threatened. The isolated cases of mutation of species or measurable levels of pollution did not appear to be affecting the basic factors that drive Lake Baikal's ecosystem. She would not dispute that all but a tiny fraction of the lake's water remains clean. And although she seemed right in a broad, commonsensical way when she said that something must be amiss if the omul are breeding badly and so on, she had no factual argument that the lake's ecosystem as a whole, its overall biological balance, was threatened.

As we spoke to her we started to develop an idea which was to become one of our project's chief conclusions: more needed to be known about the hard facts of Lake Baikal, but the local scientific community was so starved of money that it didn't seem as if a comprehensive assessment of the lake's condition was possible. Kazhova might well have been correct, indeed probably was correct, in her gloomy outlook. But without factual analysis of a highly credible and persuasive nature, her side would never be able to overcome the forces of inertia, bureaucracy, and self-interest arrayed against it. If she couldn't really convince us of her case – and we wanted to be convinced – how would she ever convince the men in Moscow, much less the twenty thousand local people depending upon the Baikalsk mill for their livelihoods?

After the expedition I came to appreciate one argument that is a powerful counterweight to the truth, effectively deployed by defenders of the status quo, that there is as yet no discernible pollution in the lake's openwater zones. (Remember that biologically there are two Baikals: the coast, or 'littoral', which is not particularly special, and the rest, the 'pillagel', which is where almost all the endemism and evolutionary interest is.) The argument rests on a tiny crustacean, a phyto-plankton called *Epishura baicalensis*, the one organism upon which the rest of Baikal's unique ecosystem might be said to rely.

In the course of their foraging, the epishura filter 450 million cubic metres of water annually, an amount equivalent to over seven times the water entering the lake. It is not only a highly effective filtering agent but also a crucial link in the food chain sustaining other filter species. Unfortunately for Baikal's survival prospects, the epishura is more sensitive to water purity than is almost any other species known to man. Even without pollution, for example, the epishura cannot live in Baikal's coastal zone. Considering this extreme sensitivity to outside influences it is no surprise that if man-made pollution were to spread beyond its current isolated littoral patches and into the pillagel, it would herald the end of this most important of cogs in Lake Baikal's ecosystem. What is the danger of this happening? Baikal is so big that the pillagel remains completely uncontaminated, for it takes a long time to sully 23,000 cubic kilometres of water. But the Baikalsk mill and other polluters are still spewing out their waste, with no end in sight, and the same hugeness that has so far protected the lake also means that once it is polluted it will not have time to purify itself before its biology is terminally deranged.

Opposite:
Siberian faces
(J.B.)

Hearing Dr Kazhova's *cries de cœur*, vague as they seemed, I felt a sense of urgency about returning to the lake. I think we all felt this. All the same we thought Irkutsk a good town as towns went. The centre of it is for the most part rather pretty, with quite a few eighteenth-century, nineteenth-century, and turn-of-the-century buildings. Many are in the neoclassical, imperial mode while others have strong oriental touches. Classic Siberian wooden architecture exists even in the heart of the city. In some places the old wooden structures, with their log or panelled walls and their ornate trim of carved and painted wood, were like little gems among the concrete Stalinist lowrises.

Irkutsk is the capital and urban soul of Siberia, a place where these contrasts are natural. The city is a provincial dowager living in two ages, a frontier entrepot and a minor metropolis, a Csarist boomtown and the plaything of Soviet directives. On the whole, Irkutsk is probably what one should expect from a nineteenth-century provincial capital at the heart of a region rich in trade and materials, in a country determined to show its wealth and prove its European character. It is formal, ambitious and pretty; and, because of where it is, a little surprising.

In the central market, humming and swirling over more than an acre, covered stalls offered technicolour pyramids of fresh fruit, pallets of vegetables and vivid hanging cuts of beef, mutton and pork. In small kiosks around the periphery, the new breed of entrepreneurs were selling Marlboros, Mars bars, cold Heineken, Boy George tapes and Stallone videos. Flowers, watermelon, oranges and tomatoes had been brought by lorry and train from Tajikistan and Uzbekistan. Families of Turkic traders tended the makeshift stalls under which they would sleep every night until their produce sold or rotted. Then they would travel their new Silk

Road back across Inner Asia, leaving the land of evergreen forests and log cabins to return to the oases and minarets of their own country.

Several months earlier, I had not been impressed when I had read that Irkutsk was the 'cultural capital of Siberia'. 'Siberia', that synonym for physical misery and moral injustice, the conventional image of an earthly hell, was not a word I had associated with 'culture'. But I was very wrong.

In the 1860s the Russian writer Nikolai Shelgunov wrote that 'Just as England created London, and France Paris, so Siberia created Irkutsk.' Pre-eminently among Siberian cities, Irkutsk was the beneficiary of the region's extraordinary cross-current of wealth, culture and adventurous attitudes. Two hundred years earlier, in the thick of the Buryat wars, a Cossack band led by Yokhav Pokhabov had chosen the confluence of the Irkut and Angara rivers as the site for a new settlement from which to extract *yasak* from the local tribes and stage further conquests east and south. Pokhabov reported to his superiors that by 1661 wooden fortifications and a barn for storing grain had been erected and the site was showing potential for future 'ploughing, hunting, haymaking and grazing'. Despite the attraction of the gold and silver thought to exist plentifully in the region, in Irkutsk's case Eldorado fantasies of easy riches were expressed by rumours of packs of sable roaming the streets wearing their furry black gold.

By the end of the seventeenth century, Irkutsk's population had grown to include 409 Cossacks, 300 artisans and petty tradesmen, 291 gentry, minor officials, peasants and exiles and one hangman. Commerce burgeoned as cartloads of wax, iron and manufactured goods from Moscow, St Petersburg, the Netherlands, England and Spain passed through the town from the West and caravans of furs, mica (cheaper for windows than glass), Chinese tea and silk headed out of Siberia for Europe.

A century later Irkutsk was the local administrative capital, and Mongolian, Chinese, Manchurian and Japanese were being taught at the Central Public School. Alexander Radishchev, often called Russia's first revolutionary, arrived in 1791, marking the start of the city's long supply of liberal aristocrats and their families. He found a city of twenty thousand inhabitants, twelve churches, a broad range of educational institutions, a museum, a theatre, banks and hospitals.

Ten years later, Alexander I succeeded his father, Paul, 'the mad Csar', on the imperial throne in St Petersburg. In Russia's new, westward-looking capital, the liberal ideals of the European Enlightenment were gaining currency with the young elite. Alexander encouraged their aspirations. Men who had fought with him against Napoleon saw themselves as liberators of a continent as constitutional governments were established in Poland and Hungary. But Alexander failed to deliver and the hopes

Opposite:
Clockwise, from top:
The Hotel Siberia

Maria Volkonskaya and
Nikolai, her first child

Four Decembrists
in their cell

of the progressive *jeunesse dorée* were turned against the state. Adding the new spirit of Romanticism to the egalitarian rationalism of their original Enlightenment ideals, they glorified sacrifice, heterodoxy and a vague, aspirational nobility of the spirit. In the decade after Waterloo they formed secret revolutionary societies with dreamers' names like Polar Star, argued the details of their various millenarian visions, and plotted assassinations and revolution.

A succession crisis following Alexander's sudden death in November of 1825 gave the revolutionaries their opportunity. On 14th December, the day when all servants of the Russian state were to swear allegiance to the new Emperor, a couple of hundred young officers, followed by a regiment of guards and an assortment of smaller units, marched on St Petersburg's Senate Square, hoping to install a constitutional monarchy in the place of Romanov autocracy. It is said that some of the officers thought that 'Constitutsiya' was the name of Grand Duke Constantine's wife. Their effort was hopelessly amateur and by the afternoon, following minor bloodshed, they had been dispersed or captured. Five of the leaders were hanged and 121 others sent to Siberia. The Decembrists, as they and their families came to be known, were to make important contributions to the city of Irkutsk and the lands around it, on both shores of Lake Baikal.

The Decembrists' wives enjoyed glittering places at the centre of St Petersburg society. When their husbands were convicted, the women were officially declared widows by the Church and state, allowing them to remarry at will should they want to retain their comfortable lives. If they chose to follow their husbands to Siberia they would have to renounce rank, titles, servants and wealth. They would have to leave their sons and daughters behind in European Russia; they would be allowed only four hours per week with their husbands, and these in the presence of an officer of the state. Any children born to them in Siberia would be state serfs. Nine of the rebels' wives decided to follow their husbands and agreed in writing to each of these conditions. Two women who were betrothed to exiled Decembrists determined to do the same, hoping that at some time in the unforeseeable future the Csar would allow them to marry. The unofficial conditions of their decision were equally appalling: a 3,500-mile journey by cart, horse, foot and sled across Siberia's lawless wastes, and their best years spent in hunger, loneliness, illness and dark discomfort.

In September of 1826, Princess Trubetskaya was the first to arrive in Irkutsk. After several weeks of bureaucratic obstruction, she was allowed a fleeting visit to her husband at his labour camp deep in the wilderness on the far side of Baikal. The eight other wives and two betrothed followed gradually. For the next decade they followed their husbands from prison to prison, travelling hundreds of miles each time, forced to find their own guides and transport and living off government rations. Trubetskaya was chased by bandits in the taiga, stranded on river ice, and her hair – the same 'curls more shining than sunlight and darker than night' once eulogised by Pushkin – frozen to the mattress on which she slept. 'What courage one needs to live in this country!' wrote Princess Volkonskaya to her mother, hostess of St Petersburg's leading literary and artistic salon. 'It is fortunate that we are forbidden to write to you frankly about it.'

Meanwhile the rebels themselves kept their minds alive. According to one historian, 'One Decembrist lectured on higher mathematics, another on chemistry and physics, and still others spoke about astronomy, history and literature... and one mastered no fewer than thirteen languages before he finished serving his sentence.' As their prison and labour sentences softened into simple exile, many of the Decembrists moved to Irkutsk itself, where their activities in the apolitical realms available to them continued to express their progressive sentiments. During their time in Siberia they had introduced new crops, found new uses for them, built churches, conducted economic surveys, hydrological studies and species counts, established scientific groups, founded quartets, libraries and theatres. The Trubetskoys' house in Irkutsk is now the Decembrist Museum. It stands on a street still named after Felix Dzerzhinsky, chief Inquisitor of the Bolshevik terror and grandfather of the KGB.

A contemporary of the Decembrists had rightly predicted that it was the destiny of their wives 'to grant history a few beautiful lines'. During our Fourth of July dinner, Sergei persuaded three young women eating nearby to join us at our table but they were not, sadly, to provide this particular story with 'a few beautiful lines'. While two of them did have rather beautiful lines of their own, the girls were of a red-lipsticked, gum-chewing, jaded type that would not have fitted well in the St Petersburg salons of Mesdames Volkonskaya and Trubetskaya. Then again, after a month on the trail and half a dozen vodka toasts, nor would we. Just as our fantasies of an Irkutsk brimming with swan-necked, ivory-skinned French-speaking Csarist beauties were sorely disappointed, I am afraid that whatever Sergei told the girls to expect of us was equally misleading. The milk-and-honey American aspirations of young Russians tended to look towards *Dallas* and we'd just staggered out of Dodge City. The girls were young, the oldest of them twenty-three and the youngest nineteen. But they were accomplished, independent businesswomen. Already they had made several trips to Cyprus with a male protector, to buy dresses and cheap bangles to sell back in Irkutsk.

95

Their Marlboros and gaudy, bespangled clothes attested to their success. The Cypriot men, they said, had been utterly charming.

These girls belonged to a breed often called the New Russians: traders and speculators, hard and certain and inarticulate. The girls looked at Genia like he was a flea-bitten old donkey. Genia looked at them with avuncular pity. These ladies weren't interested in charm. They wanted to be impressed. And how could Nikolai, a champion playboy of his generation, impress them with tales of Mustique and Klosters when they'd seen the boutiques and kebab shops of Nicosia?

We had scheduled a meeting with a couple of environmental activists in the regional parliament building on the following afternoon. The Irkutsk Regional Soviet was housed in a huge monolith of grey concrete. Appended to the exterior were a few nods to classical architecture – pilasters and the like. Taran had not been a great researcher of primary or even secondary sources at university and as we walked up those clumsy neoclassical steps John informed him that the big grey building in the middle of the Harvard campus, the one that looked a little like the Irkutsk Soviet, had been the university library.

One of the greens was a journalist called Maximov, who claimed to have written over fifty articles on ecological subjects associated with Lake Baikal. He had been taken to court for libel three times by the management of the Baikalsk mill and said that he had won all three cases by refuting the evidence of scientists with the evidence of his own senses. There was really no practical way to corroborate his claim about these successes in court. But if the claim were true, then at least the courts in Eastern Siberia were not so corrupt and beholden to powerful interests as one would have expected.

Maximov alluded boldly to Tolstoy ('scientists have no conscience'), Kant ('the sky is limitless and the human species knows no morality and therefore cannot behave criminally'), Hemingway, an obscure but insightful Italian novelist ('you can eat cheese but not gold'), and physics ('water does not boil until every drop is ready'). His argument about Baikal was that the standard of living is the real problem and that people so concerned with self-preservation cannot afford an ecological conscience. He also contended that there is no room for morality in politics, for politicians are all self-serving.

Maximov's friend, Mr Yagolin, a Deputy in the Irkutsk Soviet, disagreed. He said there were many politicians who, like himself, were motivated by a desire to serve. Mr Yagolin had filed the first action ever to be brought to court under the ecological law of 1992, which allows private citizens to bring suits against factories that break ecological laws. The case had been scheduled to be heard in late June but had been delayed until an indeterminate date in July. This seemed a good thing for Mr Yagolin, who could not cite us a single piece of data regarding public health problems or illegal waste emissions. He told us he had given all of his documents to the court and had no copies. Such a course would have been lunacy in Switzerland, much less Siberia, but Mr Yagolin was such an odd bird that he might well not have been trying to conceal from us that he had no proof at all. Anyway, he said, he didn't expect to win the case. The power of the pulp mill was too great in the region and at the Ministry of Forest Industries in Moscow.

Mr Yagolin was a pallid, crooked man, sunken-faced, nearly toothless and really quite depressing to look at. He told us on the way out of the meeting room that his forefathers had all been well over six feet tall and that he and his peers would have been big like us but for Soviet pollution. This was one of the achingly possible half-truths that often made our project very frustrating. As a result of such claims and the conflicting views and facts of the scientists we had spoken to, Russia was taking shape in our understanding as a land where paranoia, legend, and fact combined to form some opaque, coded reality.

A day later we headed back to the seismic station and our horses. We were pleased to leave. Irkutsk, so full of decent food and old churches, of bars, museums, and other human refinements, had been hell after the taiga.

chapter seven

BRIDGES AND TUNNELS OF THE TRANS-SIBERIAN

6:15 P.M., 7TH JULY, TALIA SEISMOLOGICAL STATION, SOUTHERN CORNER OF LAKE BAIKAL

We arrived here from Irkutsk at lunch time to find that Genia and the new horses have been chasing each other through the taiga at a nearby collective farm since yesterday morning. Nik, John and Sergei have gone off to find Genia and give him a hand. Taran, Kerim and I are holding the fort here.

It is a delight to see our horses again after our spell in the big city. They are not, however, looking as fat and happy after their four days' rest as we had hoped. We have moved them to new patches of grass and given them each two-thirds of a bucket of oats.

There is one new horse here, a weedy little dark grey mare. Of our old horses, one – Tofka – is absent, presumably helping Genia with the round-up. Painful memories of chasing the horses around that island after Camp Selenge make the three of us feel rather clever not to have volunteered to go find Genia in the taiga and help him with the round-up.

Opposite:
A coal pile and crane at Kultuk
(J.B.)

The wranglers did not return to camp until nine thirty that evening. Genia had found a beautiful stallion running loose in one of the collective's paddocks, a 20-acre enclosure of taiga and pasture, and after four hours of chasing and stalking they had managed to corner the beast, pacify him with a heap of oats, and rope him.

Long before they were expected back, the stew that we were cooking for them had burned and then turned into a brown volcanic cement. It was to be the last time that our Russian companions trusted us to cook anything. From that night Russians cooked and gringos washed up.

Genia and the others were so excited about the new stallion that they didn't mind having to wait for a new batch of stew. Nikolai and John told us about the horse as they took us through the woods to the grassy river bank where they had tied him up for the night. He had been galloping at the head of his herd of mares, geldings and colts in open grassland when they had first seen him. According to the head of the collective that owned him, he hadn't been ridden for three years, and then only lightly. He'd never been shod. For years since he had driven his herd's previous lead stallion into isolation, he had enjoyed the unchallenged sovereignty of his world.

When I first saw him, in a twilit streamside meadow high up there in the hills, he seemed a member of a higher species than that to which our other horses belonged. He was so haughtily alive that even as he ate he seemed to be doing what he wanted to do rather than what his nature required him to do. His brown coat had a gunmetal tinge that I had never seen before. He looked strong and lithe, but when he moved about his little meadow he did it slowly.

99

'What's his name?' Taran asked.

'Bilugubi,' said John. 'It means white lips.' It was a good name. The stallion's lips and nose were fringed with white, as if he had just been caught slurping from a milk-pail. The result was an innocent, dreamy quality that we soon learned fitted his nature perfectly.

Poor Taran had stuck himself with the dud gelding Malish, back at Camp Selenge. For his filming he needed a horse with strength and spirit. So we gave him Bilugubi and he was delighted and the rest of us were jealous.

Opposite:
Big Rizhka in a
shoeing stockade
(K.Y.)

The following morning we saddled-up for the first time in too long and on we rode. After descending from the seismic station through the taiga to Lake Baikal, just a few miles away, we passed through a grubby coal-mining town called Kultuk, which lies on the south-west corner of the crescent-shaped lake. From there on until we reached the top of the lake in late August, we would be riding north up Baikal's West Coast. The first stretch of this leg was to take us fifty miles from that southern corner to a town called Port Baikal, where the Angara River, Baikal's sole effluent, begins its journey to a junction with the mighty Yenisei and thence to the Arctic Ocean. Although this leg of the expedition was to be only fifty miles, we expected a hard time and we got one.

Shortly after riding out of Kultuk, we were heading north. Soon we rode past six long-haired Irkutsk day-trippers singing and playing a guitar. It was a sunny day and they were drinking something strong from a red plastic container. We stopped and sat down on a grassy slope facing the Sacred Sea, seven horsemen and six drunk hippies sharing a jerry-can of vodka. We were not yet far from the relatively polluted southern shore but the water was already brilliantly clear. What were the hippies doing there?

'We have come to Baikal to wash our souls,' said one.

'To rejuvenate our spirits,' added another. It was true. Only after Kultuk, with the tarmac and villages behind us, did Baikal's weather, its coastline and its wild hinterlands finally allow us to feel the lake's ghostly, uncanny force. The Buryats had sometimes called the lake Baigal, meaning 'great flame' and the exiled schismatic Avvakum had seen the bounty of its birds, fish and seals, the 'halls and turrets' of its mountains, and concluded that 'all this hath been wrought by Christ in heaven for man so that he should find pleasure in it and praise his redeemer.'[1]

Within a day the shoreline became precipitously steep, for we were at last among Avvakum's 'pillars and gates, walls and courts'. Our only way forward was to follow the decrepit train-tracks of the so-called Circum-Baikal Link, where the Trans-Siberian railway had been hewn from the cliffs which form Baikal's south-western littoral. The original

"The Usual Accident on the Great Siberian Railway"

route of the world's greatest railway had avoided this engineering nightmare by using a vast steam ferry called the *Baikal*, capable of muscling through 38 inches of ice while carrying twenty-eight loaded freight cars, to link the lake's East and West Coasts. Soon enough, seven thousand freight cars were backed up along the line and it was clear that the ferry system was not going to work. The call went up for a new way of getting to the other side, and the Circum-Baikal Link was built. Today it is used only by sporadic local trains, for the Trans-Siberian now takes a far gentler route well inland of the coastal mountains.

A writer called Harmon Tupper, whose book *To the Great Ocean* may be the best single history of the Trans-Siberian railroad, has written much about the subject. Here is his description of the building of the segment of the Circum-Baikal Link which we followed:

Much of the route was inaccessible by road and could be reached by water solely in those brief periods when Baikal was comparatively free of fog. Hurricane winds and lashing waves not only delayed operations but also necessitated miles of masonry walls to anchor the artificial embankments that had to be built up from the sinuous, rocky shoreline with an average of 101,720 cubic yards of earth and stone per mile. [The] contractors were forced to dynamite cuttings through mountain folds that fell sheer into the water, and to bore thirty-three tunnels. Inlets, gorges, and Baikal's tributaries required more than two hundred bridges and trestles.[2]

Baikal's south-west shore had been dangerous for the men building the railway, so much so that some historians have called the Circum-Baikal Link the most difficult stretch of railway ever built. Dynamiting the roadbed from the naked cliffside, carving tunnels through huge rock outcroppings, the workers died from bad explosives, rockslides, exposure, malnutrition and disease.

Of the many kinds of artisans and labourers working on the Link, it had been the bridge builders who tended to suffer most. The same had been true all along the Trans-Siberian, and in winter it was worse than ever. At one stage a workman was overheard to say, 'This ain't railroad building. It's a battle, a war to the death.' Speed was the priority, medicine unavailable, and nature deeply hostile. Rapacious contractors and venal officials ensured that materials were shoddy and safety procedures ignored. Our part of the Link – from Kultuk to Port Baikal – was built at the cost of 'a record-breaking $216,000 per mile'. Among other problems, the first test train suffered ten derailings on these fifty-two miles.[3]

Eighty-nine years after they were built, many of the bridges consisted in places of nothing but battered ties laid across skeletal wooden structures. On our third day on the tracks, Sarge very nearly came to a messy

Opposite:
Above:
A landslide on the
Circum-Baikal link

Below:
From *The Great Siberian
Railway*

end on such a bridge when, high above a rocky gorge, he crashed to his belly through gaps between the ties. In a plunging, adrenal rush, neighing mightily, he struggled up and scrambled across the rest of the fifteen-yard bridge. Reaching safety on the far side he stopped and stood almost motionless on his cut and bruised legs, the sound of his breathing beating a fast, tremulous tattoo. I checked the cuts on his legs to be sure that the damage was superficial, tied him to a tree and returned to the others by foot. We spent the next four hours seeking a way to bring the other horses down the cliff, swimming them between the boulders where the gorge meets the lake, and scrambling them back up the other side.

Opposite:
Taran at the end of
a tunnel
(J.B.)

We couldn't use torches in the railway tunnels because the shadows spooked the horses. In the damp and utter blackness, unable to see the horses between our legs, with only the pressure of foot against stirrup to guide our balance, grinding against unseen rough-hewn rock walls and fallen wood braces, coaxing our mounts and dragging our pack-horses, we prayed that one of the four daily trains, their schedules impossible to predict, would not come rattling through.

On our second day on the tracks, Piotr hit the bottle once more. His last two days in Irkutsk had been written off by a binge following our Fourth of July party. Slouching in his saddle and gibbering like a baboon, he whipped his horse and those nearby into a dangerous trot. I caught him up and grabbed his reins. We were soon within one notch of self-restraint from coming to blows on our horses. The next morning, when he had sobered up, I docked him three days' pay. It was difficult. He was a small man physically but he was tough, good in the taiga, and a genius with an axe. He was energetic and had been good at arranging meetings and interviews. A day later he was drunk again.

After six weeks in the saddle we were more intent than ever upon getting around the lake before the September storms and October snows made Baikal's savage coastline impassable. The expedition had settled into a hard, driven attitude and we all knew that thus far, on the easiest part of the route, we had already been lucky to escape disaster on several occasions. We had seven hundred miles of wilderness ahead of us. I steeled my nerve, gathered a meeting, and dressed Piotr down formally and severely, docking him five more days' pay.

Genia smoked and stared at the ground as I spoke. Deputy head of a sable-trapping collective, a true taiga man, straight and solid, he had earned among us a respect that meant his views on foolishness never needed articulation. Sergei shared with his famous father a keen empathy for the Russian character, its earthiness, sentimentality, and sense of its own sacred uniqueness. He had developed a protective instinct towards Piotr, a generous, dishonest, hopelessly Russian man. Piotr responded to my words with a few deflecting platitudes about teamwork but essentially he took it on the chin. Sergei translated with a trembling upper lip and a pained blinking of the eyes.

The next day we rode into a settlement called Maritui, a chocolate-box alpine village lying in one of the few tiny, habitable valleys along the southern West Coast. In the spring of 1901, Maritui had become the temporary home of a man called Alexander Pertsov as he started the project that was to make him one of the heroes of railroad history, 'a dynamic architect and civil engineer who preferred hard jobs to easy ones'. Having been assigned the task of linking Kultuk and Port Baikal with the final fifty-two of the Trans-Siberian's epic six thousand miles of track, Pertsov (according to the railway historian Tupper)

dug in at Maritui, about halfway between Port Baikal and Kultuk, for a protracted assault in both directions againt the worst sector, comprising fifty-odd miles of precipitous cliffs broken by capes, ravines, bays, and narrow shelvings. With him in a spacious new log house were his wife and children, and, quartered in nearby barracks, a labour force of somewhat less than ten thousand Russian, Turkish, Persian and Italian workers...[4]

We were unable to ascertain whether the dynamic Pertsov's 'spacious new log house' still stood in Maritui, but we did have the welcome surprise of meeting the Vice Director of Irkutsk University's Institute of Geography. He was in the village with a few of his graduate students, doing fieldwork as part of his Institute's mission to study land use in the lake's watershed. We spoke to him for about an hour on the rocky beach between Baikal and the sparse pastureland and dark, unpainted log houses of the settlement. His name was Professor Snytko, a bright and likable man. His chief interest was how man should use Baikal.

We asked him what Baikal's biggest problems were.

'Do you see these cement breakwaters here? They represent a problem that does not get talked about as much as the other "monsters" of Baikal. I mean the construction of the hydroelectric dam on the Angara, which has raised the lake's water level.' His words called to my mind a chilling recollection by the Irkutsk poet and essayist Mark Sergeyev. When the Angara was first dammed in 1959, Sergeyev had watched with a patriotic pride that he later regretted as the last 25-ton boulders were dropped into the river bed by trucks painted with the inscription 'We will conquer you, Angara!'

'This dam', continued Professor Snytko, 'has disturbed the biological life of Baikal, creating erosion and swamping spawning grounds. Of course, some people argue that the water level changes anyway, but the natural fluctuations occur over geological time and this 1-metre rise during a short period has been very dramatic.'

'What about the towns and villages?'

'Well, we live as if in the stone age here on Baikal, so ordinary people cannot do much harm. People live in terrible conditions. You can feel that even here in this little village.

'The Selenge River, I believe, is the biggest source of pollution. It gathers all the filth in northern Mongolia and most of Buryatia and brings it to Baikal. The second monster is the Baikalsk mill, which should never have been built. And the third monster, in a broad sense, is the railroads: the Trans-Siberian along the South Coast and the Baikal-Amur Mainline, which touches the northern tip. Whether or not we want to admit it, there are accidents on these railroads and waste from these accidents enters the lake. There has been more than one oil spill. This, however, is a monster we can fight.

'But to fight the Selenge and to fight Baikalsk, that is more difficult. Last year we had more of the old rumours: they forbade this, they stopped that. And now everything still goes on, worse than ever. We created a city at Baikalsk. Not a big city, but a city. Close the mill now and everybody will ask what will the people do? This is the eternal problem on Baikal: people have to live together with the lake and not just use it.

'If the pollution continues the mineral balance will be upset, deranging the food chain. Baikal is full of different kinds of life, from zooplankton, sponges and fish up to the Baikal seal, the nerpa. Everything has existed in undisturbed friendship for many years. And now many things disturb the food chain. You probably heard about the mass deaths of nerpa in 1990. That was like a warning of nature: that even the Csar of Baikal – the nerpa – feels all these changes.'

I asked what he had to say to those who, like Dr Pavlov at the Institute of Toxicology, contend that there is no pollution anywhere in Baikal below a depth of 50 metres. The lake's maximum recorded depth is 1,647 metres. Less than 1 per cent of the water is in the top 50 metres.

'Pavlov's Institute was created in order to justify the Baikalsk pulp mill. They have always tried to prove that nothing disturbs Baikal, that nothing can destroy it. I once had a graduate student from the Institute of Toxicology and her point of view was completely different from that of the Institute's administration. They publish their papers saying that nothing is happening with Baikal, that harmful substances cannot be found everywhere, that there are some clean areas. But none of this is true. It is easy to say that everything is OK.

'As well as the lake itself, the health of the watershed that feeds it is an important factor. As a scientist once said, so long as there is taiga there will be a Baikal. So if there will be a normal environment, normal usage of nature in the basin of the Selenge, then things will be OK and we can finally talk about saving Baikal.'

'So what needs to be done?'

'Personal attitudes are very important. If the people feel that they are the owners of the land, then they will treat the lake accordingly, as if it and the land were their home. But unfortunately at this moment when the economic situation is so difficult and so loose people want to enrich themselves and they don't think much about ecology.'

Opposite:
Taran doing the dishes
(J.B.)

I said that we had heard talk of privatising Baikalsk.

'We should not allow the privatisation of factories around Baikal. Maybe some time in the future we should do this, but not now. If we put these factories in private hands under our present economic system there will be no restraints. And Baikalsk itself, if it is ever privatised, there will be no way to close it.'

In the background some students were singing that old Russian folk-song, 'Sacred Baikal – glorious sea; an old omul barrel – my glorious ship...'

I asked Snytko to whom he felt the lake belonged, for some Russians worried about a loss of sovereignty that might accompany Baikal's proposed designation as a UNESCO World Heritage Site.

'A lake belongs to the state. But in a broader sense I would say that it belongs to mankind. It belongs to you, to me, to him.' He pointed at an old man fishing off the rocks with a simple pole and lure. 'To everybody.'

'So what can the international community do to help Russia save Baikal?'

'It is very difficult to say. But the West helped us to create this "miracle",' he said, gesturing across the water towards the faint brown pall hanging over Baikalsk. 'We used a Finnish purifying system, at the time the most modern one in the world. They gave us this system and said that we would be OK, but it turns out that we are not OK. That's why any project is risky. You have to be very rational and very careful in treating any part of nature. And with Baikal you have to think twenty times before doing something.'

'But now that it's all happened, what should be done?'

'To do little charitable things is not so difficult. Everybody likes to do that. You like to help people, I like to help people. But to speak about more serious things on the level of the state? It's just a joke to make such plans. Remember, the people of the watershed live off the lake. Baikal gives them food, water, jobs. Yet still they pollute it. How much help can we expect if we fail to show the will ourselves? Just as Russia and the West cannot settle things in Yugoslavia, so it is for you here.'

That evening three men in a rowing boat stopped at the beach where we had piled our saddles and set a fire for the night's camp. After a tense, hot day in the saddle, Kerim and I were swimming. The air was still warm. The evening sky was cloudless and our beach of smooth grey pebbles reached out platinum and cool into the calm azure water. One of the three men wore a pistol on his hip and another, shirtless and violently fit, was wearing camouflage trousers and a green beret.

Opposite:
Genia with Karka and
Little Rizhka
(J.B.)

They were policemen, they said, a riot squad of sorts from the Sludyanski District Police Department. Their leader was a twenty-three-year-old Azeri. It was hard to believe that this pistol-toting crowd-taming cop, with his hard confidence and three-inch cheek-bone scar, was the same age as me.

'What are you doing so far from home?' I asked. He might well have wanted to ask the same question. Even in his childhood in Azerbaijan, he said, he'd heard about the Sacred Sea and its problems. There was to be dancing at Maritui that evening and the policemen were going back to keep the peace. Ninety years earlier our Azeri friend, however tough he looked, would have needed more than two companions to do the job. In the years 1901–4, when Pertsov and his family were sharing Maritui with 'somewhat less than ten thousand Russian, Turkish, Persian and Italian workers', the town's population had also included 'a garrison of tough Circassian guards to break up brawls, patrol whorehouses, and intercept bootleggers, predominantly women who wrapped up jugs of vodka to resemble swaddled babies'.[5]

1   Avvakum, A. (1960) *The Life of Archpriest Avvakum by Himself*, trans. V. Nabokov, New York.
2   Tupper, H. (1965) *To the Great Ocean: Siberia and the Trans-Siberian Railway*, Boston.
3   Ibid.
4   Ibid.
5   Ibid.

chapter eight

THE WEST COAST

AT the end of the train-tracks we reached the large village of Port Baikal, where between 1900 and 1905 the ferry *Baikal*, three hundred feet long, powered by three 1,250-horsepower engines feeding off five boilers each, all of it built and disassembled at Newcastle-upon-Tyne before being sent to Listvyanka in sections, had taken on and disgorged her cargoes of freight cars before the building of the Circum-Baikal Link.

Port Baikal is situated where the lake spills over its banks to become the Angara River, a turbulent stream as big as all of Baikal's 336 tributaries combined and as powerful as European Russia's four largest rivers (the Volga, Kama, Don and Dnieper) put together. At the point where it cuts through Baikal's steep mountain walls, the Angara is less than a mile wide and so deep and fast that it was not bridged until 1936. When we rode into Port Baikal, the ferry across to Listvyanka had made its last scheduled run but we persuaded the ferryman to make a special trip for the *expeditsy ecologisky Tamerlan*.

A breeze blew up ten minutes into the crossing and the horses scraped and sprawled over the fifty-foot *Babushkin*'s steel decks as we steamed across the choppy Angara. We disembarked at Listvyanka and rode north along its nineteenth-century seaside promenade for half a mile before turning left into the taiga to make camp for the night. The lovers and grannies of Listvyanka walked slowly past us along the promenade, taking the sea air as the cast-iron lamplights glowed orange in the summer twilight.

Sergei caught the romantic mood, riding into town for a sundown tryst with a sixteen-year-old girl he had met as we first rode through. Nik and I joined him and had a good canter back. In the morning when Sergei arrived for breakfast, he looked enigmatic and a little tired. The rest of us, during the two days that we spent resting the horses in a meadow in the bush inland of the town, had to get our excitement from a visit to the Listvyanka offices of Irkutsk's Limnological Institute. Limnology is the study of fresh-water bodies, especially lakes.

There a man called Dr Fialkov explained what was to us a new vision of Baikal. We had already heard about Baikal the Reservoir, the Job Provider, the Cleanser of Souls. It was Fialkov who introduced us to the notion of Baikal the Classroom. He saw Baikal as a holistic macrocosm on a scale that was just right for teaching the world how geology, chemistry and biology interact. And Baikal's isolation, deep in pristine forest a thousand miles from any other sea or ocean, had allowed the biological developments created by its other physical attributes to unfold unaffected by external influences. Unlike the Galapagos Islands, where a sort of

parallel evolution occurred in remote but unremarkable physical circumstances, in Baikal's open water and depths the entire ecosystem, the whole web of life, is utterly unique and self-evolved.

Giving all of this further potential as a teaching tool was the fact that for the moment Baikal continues to function well in its natural ways. It is still the cleanest place on earth, with pollution levels comparable to those in the Arctic. Baikal needed to be preserved, he said, because of what it could teach not only the men with microscopes but all of us.

The wondrous spectacle of Baikal's sponges, seals, and translucent golomyanka, that extraordinary fish which gives birth to live young and is so fatty that it melts in the sunlight, tells a tale about how the physical world shapes life, how species evolve, and how living things depend upon each other. The cases of mutation and falling species counts show us how man can make it go wrong. The biological and chemical purity of its water and the old Buryat methods of fishing and nerpa hunting show us how Baikal could sustain us eternally. And the beauty of the place, so potent that all who have felt it have recognised something holy, gives these lessons a weight that makes it all matter in a realm deeper than that of knowledge and theory.

Fialkov talked about giving visitors a combination of physical experience of Baikal and actual teaching by the scientists who study it. He had a vision of cruises accompanied by scientists and lecturers and backed up with events at his Institute, which is home to an impressive collection of displays and teaching facilities. A crucial part of Fialkov's concept was Baikal's accessibility. By boat, as he said, 'every child and grandmother can travel into the heart of a wilderness, probably the only one they will ever see.' And, as he pointed out, it was no steamy, disease-ridden jungle. Visitors to Baikal would never be jolted for hours in Land Rovers, catch malaria, and sweat so much they couldn't think. There was no doubt that the lake's summer climate is a world-class restorative. After a day and a half on a boat heading north from Irkutsk, any healthy seventy-year-old could be looking out at a coastline as wild as any on earth, deriving all the liberating benefits of such a sight, and learning all the while about biology, evolution and ecology. The same could be said of school-children and everybody in between. I found Fialkov's vision a potent one and could not help thinking that it revealed the sort of big heart and creative mind that Baikal needed among its protectors.

The next morning we saddled-up again and rode on north. Four hundred miles of the West Coast's steep, rocky shoreline and largely untracked taiga awaited us. Before riding out of our camp in the bush behind Listvyanka, we fried some sausage we'd bought in town. An hour later Rasputin seemed to be throwing one of his legendary

Opposite:
Above:
The ice-breaking
steam-driven train ferry
Baikal

Below:
Listvyanka in the old days

debauches in my innards. I clung ignominiously to my pommel until we stopped for lunch and then I tied Sarge to a tree and collapsed onto the taiga floor.

Piotr scrambled off into the bush while I lay on the ground and the others cooked their lunch over a small fire twenty feet away. I looked up at the high green vaults above me, at the shafts of sunlight threading down, and smiled as I recalled another writer's description of the deep taiga as 'sepulchral'. Five minutes later, Piotr returned with some roots in his hand. Sergei translated. 'It is the podan root. Piotr says you will be better in two hours.' Piotr brewed up a batch of podan tea and told me to drink it. It went down in two gulps, so foul and bitter it had to be medicinal. I hauled myself back onto Sarge and we carried on down the trail. Two hours later the podan police had dispersed Rasputin's little party.

Opposite:
A few days north of Listvyanka
(K.Y.)

I asked Kerim if he fancied a canter. He looked at me as if I were insane, kicked his horse into a trot and off we went. A few minutes later we emerged from the taiga into a small clearing atop a cliff. Below us Baikal stretched out to the horizons like an ocean. I felt almost as good as new. Piotr's taiga-man brew, a good rolling lope through the woods on a fresh horse and a whiff of that sea breeze had done the trick.

For the next few weeks, the taiga was excruciating. Imagine a place where trees – fir, pine, spruce, cedar, alder, larch, birch and more – have been growing and falling wantonly for millennia. Fill it with bogs, mosquitoes and bear, with poisonous plants, snakes and spiders. Cover the holes between fallen trees with moss and ferns. Lay the whole thing over a chaos of mountains, ravines, boulders, crevasses and rivers. Now try to ride one horse and drag another through it all. Day in and day out, this was our experience in the bush around Lake Baikal. On the West Coast, where this 'sepulchral forest' seemed especially thick, two of us usually went ahead on foot with axes to choose, clear and blaze a trail. The taiga is beautiful and wild and quiet and it offers game, berries, wild onions and mushrooms, but it felt like our enemy.

The shore was largely composed of cliffs, boulders and sharp stones and it was often more difficult and dangerous than the taiga. The water was cold and the boulders ran straight from the steep shore into the lake. It was often tense as our horses, surprisingly bad swimmers, struggled in the deep water, bucking like rodeo broncs among submerged rocks the size of armchairs. At night we camped on thin beaches or in forest clearings. In the alpine uplands the brief summer flowerings – delphinium, astors, edelweiss, forget-me-nots, wild roses, fireweed, cinquefoil and buttercups – added colour and a welcome delicacy to what was often a hostile landscape.

Among all that tomblike taiga of the West Coast are a few arid pockets of prairie, the Buryat Steppe. In these flat and grassy places we occasionally passed shrines and holy mountains sacred to Borhan, Buddhist god of the Buryats. Borhan is an angry deity with a particular distaste for travellers, who must propitiate him with offerings of money, petty belongings, coloured cloth or vodka. The latter seemed to have been favoured by our predecessors, entailing as it did the drinking of most of the bottle before the appropriate swig or two could be left for Borhan. The holy places were marked with oboo, stands of wood posts to which the coloured cloth offerings were often tied.

Opposite:
Piotr prepares the podan root
(K.Y.)

The worshippers, so-called Western Buryats, had originally been the Bulagat, Ekherit and Khongodor Mongol tribes. They had assumed elements of their own identity after migrating around Baikal's southern tip in the thirteenth century and displacing the less warlike Tungus and other local tribes. With less steppeland in which to graze herds and range to new pastures, many of these Western Buryats became more sedentary than their Eastern cousins. They took up the cultivation of crops and their octagonal gers were often walled and roofed with wooden boards rather than felt. As with the Eastern Buryats, Genghis had failed to conquer them in several campaigns, managing only to drive them further north.

As Lamaist Buddhism spread north into Buryatia in the late sixteen hundreds, a century after it had replaced shamanism in Mongolia, it took much stronger root among the Eastern Buryats, with their closer links to Mongolia and the Mongol way of life, than among their cousins west of Baikal. A 1907 Russian encyclopedia claimed that 'the eastern Buryats, in contrast with their shamanist cousins west of Lake Baikal, were said to be milder, more peacable and restrained in character.' Shamanism is said to continue to exist among the Buryat in the lands west of Baikal, but we recognised no evidence of it. What little of it persists is believed to survive in a much-degenerated form compared with the days when the shaman's selection, rites, clothing and accessories were all part of a rigorous and highly evolved liturgy. The Buryat shaman candidate would belong to one or more of a variety of classifications. There were first-generation shamans as well as the hereditary sort, real ones and false ones, white and black. The latter were associated with West and East, respectively, and, for their pains, were obliged to 'fight with each other, hurling axes at one another from distances of hundreds of miles',[1] according to a Miss M. A. Czaplicka of Somerville College, Oxford, writing in 1914.

After all this, the unfortunate black shamans were lumped with the ability to visit death and sickness upon their fellow men. As a result,

Czaplicka relates, 'They are not liked, but much feared, by the people, who sometimes kill black shamans.'[2] This was not the only occupational hazard. For a shaman who achieved the ninth degree of consecration, the attendant responsibilities were so great that the gods tended to be 'very severe, and punish his faults or mistakes with death.'[3] Many who received the calling were reluctant to take it up. Some rejected it altogether.

Apart from the occasional oboo, we saw little evidence of the old Buryat ways. Whereas the West Coast's isolated islands of open grassland had originally been attractive to the Buryats, semi-nomadic herdsmen that they were, the collectivisation imposed by Lenin had made the traditional life far more difficult and the sedentary life of towns and permanent villages soon took over. The West Coast's pockets of steppeland gradually emptied of humans as the herding life died out.

One evening in early August we rode through an old village of about fifty wooden houses. Four families of Buryats remained. It was as if the plague had passed through. The simple wooden buildings were mostly in decent structural shape. All had lost their windows and a few were leaning into the permafrost. The only tree in town, a small apple tree in an overgrown garden, was dead. All around in the valley floor the grass was long and rich, waiting for the horses and cattle to return.

Just before mid-August the time came for Nikolai to say goodbye. He didn't want to leave us but a good job was waiting for him in New York. In those last few days with us his usually cheery demeanour took on a wistful air. It was clear, clearer than he wanted it to be, that real life was knocking hard at his door.

On the night before a scheduled passing of a hydrofoil bound southwards from Severo Baikalsk to Irkutsk, we met up with our supply ship, ominously named the *Anubis*, and our old friend Dr Yukhnin. The following morning, the *Anubis* would take Nikolai out into the middle of the lake, intercept the hydrofoil, and deposit him thereon for the first stage of his journey home to Amsterdam and thence New York and the grown-up world of suits and ties.

1:25 P.M., 10TH AUGUST, CAPE BOLSHOYE KOCA, WEST COAST OF LAKE BAIKAL

Nikolai is leaving tomorrow. All during this morning's ride, we have been thinking about what he will eat when he gets to Amsterdam. His first stop will be the local bakery, for a loaf of fresh white bread; then on to the butcher for roast beef.

The thought of this has sent us into a frenzy of food fantasies: scrambled eggs and bacon, a pink filet mignon with fresh green beans, a grilled ham and cheese sandwich with chutney and mayonnaise, ice-cream sundaes, a nice greasy bacon cheeseburger, muffins and raspberry jam, the buttery tail of a boiled lobster. We are presently enjoying a lunch of Bulgarian baked beans and dried bread crumbs.

Nikolai catches his last fish
(K.Y.)

Opposite:
Ghost Town
(J.B.)

8:50 P.M. 10TH AUGUST, SAME PLACE AND DAY

We are all tarted up for Nik's farewell dinner, resplendent in clean shirts and bandanas, leather waistcoats and shaved faces. Dr Yukhnin is overseeing the preparations of a special feast of fried potatoes and soup. Scotch, Georgian brandy, vodka and seven beers await, courtesy of the Anubis. The horses are chomping merrily away around us, the tents are set up, the fire is crackling. We are writing postcards and notes for Nik to forward from Amsterdam.

7:30 P.M., 11TH AUGUST, KOVARIZHKA, WEST COAST OF LAKE BAIKAL

We did our best at giving old Nik the mother of all goodbye parties but it didn't work. The Dutchman is still with us. The dinner started quietly with a superb soup cooked by Dr Yukhnin himself: jarred beets, cabbage and carrots, fresh onion, tomato paste, potatoes, and mayo on the side, to be dunked by the spoonful into one's mug. Nik led off the toasts with a nice greasy one to Yukhnin and the excellence with which he gathered the Russian half of our team. He was kind enough to mention his confidence that in these capable hands we would get to Babushkin one day.

Yukhnin then drank to Nik, whom he and our other Russkis had come to regard as 'a close friend, or even a relative'. And after that the deluge. When the beer and whisky and brandy were gone, plastic Finnish 'Mehikatti' orange-drink jugs started to appear, full of vodka.

We learned about the Georgian who came to Moscow and was told that 'in principle there is all the food one might ever want in Russia', and got lost looking for a store called Princip. And then there was the interesting case of 'Man comes to home, he finds other man with wife – situation traditional – and later he has little court case. Man says "I was in kitchen and wife fell on knife. Eight times."'

Dr Yukhnin leaped to his feet to recite 'Soviet Passport', a seminal work of the nationalist poet-legend Mayakovsky. Yukhnin delivered it with the thundering voice, fierce looks and slashing arms that normally accompany the classics of travel-document literature. We chanted Nikolai's name and banged our cups around for a while, then tried to fire flares into the air. Luckily most were duds and those that weren't fired straight. John kept even the Russians enthralled with a declamation of 'The Shooting of Dan McGrew' in a superb goldminer's accent accompanied by wild physical depictions of the action. Genia, blessed with a similar degree of virtuosity in the field of obscenities, led us through some of his favourite cussing sequences. All the while, the orange jugs of hooch went around and around.

I awoke on the beach at seven thirty this morning. It had rained quite hard earlier in the night and John, Kerim, Taran and I awoke in soaking sleeping bags. Nik had somehow made his way into a tent, where he slept in all his clothes, his boots, and his sleeping bag. Being fully clad must have stood him in good stead during the three quick exits he had to make from the tent during the night.

Around the breakfast fire, Boris Shishkin, captain of the Anubis, *accused us of looking like Buryats. Whether this is because we could not open our eyes or because we were stumbling around half-drunk, I do not know.*

As the Anubis *and its Dutch cargo chugged out into the lake, the hydrofoil came into sight from the north, heading south to Irkutsk. The hydrofoil, the name 'Comet' emblazoned on its hull, blazed straight on south, ignoring the sirens and flares of our little river boat.*

Poor Nik had worked hard to give himself the biggest hangover of us all, to keep him company on the eight-hour hydrofoil ride. He got a six-hour horseback ride instead. Borhan smiled on us and we had our easiest trail yet: a flat, pebbly beach the whole way, for eighteen miles. The rocks kept trotting to a merciful minimum but were not so large or sharp that we had to lead the horses.

The *Comet* was due to head south again a few days later. We met Dr Yukhnin and the *Anubis* on a rocky beach, lunched on the last of the many good pike and perch that Nik had caught for us, said goodbye to our buddy and rode off up a steep hill and into the bush. The next day he made it onto the *Comet* and, as he told us a couple of months later, ate eight Snickers bars and played Nintendo with the Captain.

I felt his departure in a way I hadn't expected. I'd known that I'd miss his company. But what I actually felt was far more practical. An hour after we'd ridden up into the taiga and left him waving at us from the beach. I realised he had been not only our strongest source of tactical advice on matters such as Bazra and Piotr but also a crucial steadying influence. When I became harsh or stubborn it was usually Nik who managed to set me straight.

3:30 P.M., 14TH AUGUST, BAIKALSKAYA, WEST COAST OF LAKE BAIKAL

We are camped in what during less dry summers would be the marshy estuary of the Ryelb River, in front of the trim village of Baikalskaya. The Anubis *has sailed north to Nizhny Angarsk, a big village at Baikal's northern tip. The ride from here to there will be about forty miles, our final stretch of this long West Coast haul. Yesterday we covered a huge thirty miles through some thick taiga. Before setting off we had packed for speed, wrapping the food, tea-pot and pans in soft gear such as tarpaulins and sleeping bags.*

At one stage, at the foot of a long hill, we stopped to prospect a way through a big bog. The blueberries were already out but the bears had been there before us and hadn't left much. After leading the horses plunging and rearing through the swamp we found an overgrown trail and followed it, bursting into short trots of a few yards wherever we found a relatively open stretch. We were flying, powering our way through log falls, dancing around stumps and boulders. Every little lead we chose happened to be the right one, every hunch of where to go when the trail died out was rewarded.

We stopped for lunch in the dark damp taiga and our satisfaction unlocked previously dormant brainpower, prompting a stunning culinary discovery that was to alter our lives significantly: we warmed our tinned beef and tinned beans together in the saucepan, rather than warming the beans separately in their tins. It is astounding what four Harvard graduates can come up with in but a couple of months of intellectual cross-fertilisation.

After lunch we carried on north up and over the watershed of the river valley we had been following. High up on the ridge we had a stirring view of rows and rows of mountains, stretching away towards Europe like the waves of an infinite green sea. All the way west to the Urals, cut by the mighty Yenisei and Lena and Ob Rivers, each of them larger and longer than the Mississippi, was the great Siberian forest, bearing in its breast oil and gold, sable and musk deer, crystal trout streams and noxious bogs, miners, loggers, reindeer herders and fur-trappers, grey little wooden camps by lakes, urban sores with names like Tomsk and Omsk, and the ghosts of a whole archipelago of gulags.

This was our first real view outside Baikal's basin. Descending the other side of the ridge, heading back through the forest towards Baikal, we emerged after a few slow hours into a series of hayfields. The fields had been scythed recently – the summer really is over – and clusters of men and women of many ages were raking the hay into heaps. After a series of canters and gallops in the late golden light, rolling side by side through the hay-nippled fields and the clusters of trees between them, we reached Baikalskaya in an hour and a quarter.

The *Anubis* awaited, with a big bucket of Dr Yukhnin's Worpi soup. We tethered the horses to the rusting hulks of ships propped up on the ground by the dock and tucked in. After supper, Yukhnin gave me a note that Nik had written that morning, as the *Anubis* was racing out, late again, to take him to the *Comet*.

Overleaf:
Left:
River crossing
(K.Y.)

Right:
The Buryat Steppe
(K.Y.)

Dear Friends [wrote Nikolai],
I did not realize just how serious our expedition was until I saw you climb that mountain and disappear into the taiga. It was an awesome sight and it hurt to know it was over for me. It was strangely moving to see the expedition as locals must see it. I wish you all a safe and exciting adventure down the East Coast. Last night we broke into the banya at the ranger station – Dr Y through the window. Admiral Boris was so drunk that he fell between the boat and the dock and I had to pull him out. Dr Y hid the bottle of Chivas somewhere – half gone!
Get it back.
Love, Nikolai

Opposite:
Harvesting in the Baikalskaya collective
(K.Y.)

We awoke the following morning to find Genia in a raging fury. Piotr had arranged for the *Anubis* to sail off taking the horseshoes we need-ed and leaving Genia without socks and cigarettes. Genia smoked con-stantly. He is smoking in almost every photograph we have of him. In the mornings he used to unzip the bottom of his tent's door-zipper and stick his head out for a smoke, groaning and harrumphing in a long steady rumble, before doing anything else. And anything other than the putrid, tube-tipped *papyrus* favoured by Russian working men was unsmokable. That morning his entire world had fallen down.

He flew into a raging tirade about all sorts of things and ended by announcing that the horses were done for, on the verge of death, frankly. They needed four or five days' rest. Preferably right here, in fact. Luckily we had no food and little fodder and there wasn't much in the village, so this wasn't an option. We fussed around the camp and stayed out of Genia's way until somebody rode into Baikalskaya and managed to buy a couple of packs from the villagers. Genia calmed down and we saddled up for the long, boring ride to Severo-Baikalsk.

Just below Baikal's northern tip, Severo-Baikalsk is a twenty-year-old town built according to blue-prints prepared by the Leningrad Zonal Research Institute of Experimental Planning. Huge toyland monuments to the heroes who built the town proclaim instead the sinister infantil-ism of the Soviet aesthetic. The people seem to know that they and their town simply should not be there, stuck in the middle of a vast per-mafrost wilderness with almost nothing to do but be their own wretched service economy. They have no industry, no mines, no agriculture, only the Baikal-Amur Mainline railway, or BAM, a railway that runs north of and broadly parallel to the Trans-Siberian, from Central Siberia, five hundred miles to the west, to the Pacific.

The BAM was originally mooted in 1904 and the first serious route proposal was made public in 1924. Japanese troops had not left Siberian soil until 1922, and the young Bolshevik state was keenly aware of the softness of its huge eastern underbelly. Siberia's natural wealth was also an issue. In 1926, speaking at the first Siberian Congress of Writers, the author Vladimir Zazubrin said of the plan:

Let the crumbling green bosom of Siberia be clad in the cement armour of cities, armed with the stone muzzles of factory chimneys, and fettered with the close-fitting hoops of railways. Let the taiga be burnt and chopped down, let the steppe be trampled under foot... It is only on cement and iron that the fraternal union of all peoples, the iron fraternity of all mankind, will be built.[4]

In 1940 the first plan for the entire route was published. Planners estimated that 285 million cubic metres of earthworks and 618,000 tons of metal bridging would be required. Even by Soviet standards this was a mammoth undertaking. Work proceeded fitfully until the so-called BAM Zone received a brief amnesty with Stalin's death in 1953. In the late 1960s, tensions with China revived the military argument for the BAM. Soaring raw materials prices in the early 1970s focused Brezhnev's attention on the strategic potential lying unmined beneath the Siberian taiga, and in 1974 serious work recommenced. BAM workers started to populate Severo-Baikalsk in that year and by 1980 the monstrous civic fancies of the Leningrad Zonal Research Institute of Experimental Planning had risen on the banks of the world's reservoir.

In 1989, the BAM became fully operational along its entire length and the full disaster was confirmed. Toxic spillage and systemic pollution degraded the local environment. The BAM and its four spurs are used by a paltry twelve trains daily, travelling at an average speed that is between a third and a quarter of that achieved by the Trans-Siberian. It is faster and safer to send goods from Japan to Europe by sea, from Hong Kong to Europe by the railways of China and Central Asia. The BAM was essentially still-born as a trans-continental freight route and Severo-Baikalsk's population of thirty thousand has been let down.

We met with the Director of Severo-Baikalsk's sewage plant and a morning touring his main facility convinced us that most of the town's sewage is quite thoroughly treated. At the end of our inspection we came to the tanks where the treated water is stored before being spewed into Baikal through a pipe. The Director drew a glass beaker of water from a tap on one of the tanks and passed it around so that we could admire its clarity. It was pretty clear, though not crystalline. But was it biologically clean? Would he, for example, drink from the beaker I held? He wasn't thirsty.

We had to stop at three or four traffic lights as we rode through Severo, queuing up for the green light among dying Ladas and belching lorries.

We rode down the wide streets and through the forests of Cold War apartment blocks looming up all around us. At last we passed into the far outskirts and found ourselves riding along Baikal again. On the lakeward fringe of the city we passed a few enormous vehicles, earth-movers, tunnel excavators and the like, that had been painted in garish kindergarten colours and raised high upon vast concrete plinths. I thought of the rhetoric that had accompanied Baikal's biggest industrial projects – 'Baikal must work', 'We will conquer you Angara', 'Let the crumbling green bosom of Siberia be clad in the cement armour of cities' and so on. The juxtaposition of monumental tractors and Sacred Sea was part of an unusual semiotic tradition.

Opposite:
Kerim making breakfast
(B.B.)

We stopped to camp in a clearing just off a rocky beach. The lake water was oily, the BAM itself was less than a hundred yards away and an abominable smell of putrefying flesh littered the air. After the wild beauty we had been living with, after seeing only the tiniest sprinklings of humanity, all of whom had adapted to nature and knew they were the junior party, the place felt sordid.

Washing the dishes after breakfast the next morning, I noticed that the stench was even stronger on the stony beach than it had been by our fire. I walked a little farther down the beach and discovered the week-old carcass of what at the best of times had been a scrawny dog, a creature all the more awful for having been white. The gulls had eaten a hole through its side the size of a saucer.

Happy to put the stench and the BAM pioneers behind us, we rode on up the coast to Nizhny Angarsk, the last settlement on the West Coast. Situated at the corner of the West Coast and the sandy river delta that links it to the East Coast, Nizhny is a delightful contrast to the concrete decrepitude of Severo-Baikalsk. It is long and thin, an overgrown village stretched on a narrow plain between the Baikalski Mountains and the shingle coastline of the lake. The only Severo-like thing about it is the hospital, built in 1976 and shut down in 1993, the year of our visit, because repairs could not keep up with the rate at which it was sinking into the marshy permafrost. Resting the horses for a couple of days before making our way across to the East Coast, we camped in the boggy stretch of ground between the village and the lake. As with many of our camps on the West Coast, the stony beach rose up to form a rampart between grassland and water.

On our first day in Nizhny Angarsk, John and I went shopping for food. As we cruised the aisles in search of treasure, I paused for a moment to observe him from the perspective of a local housewife. His filthy khaki clothes, torn and stinking and covered in layers of grime, his leather boots, six-inch blade knife, short hair, unusually tall stature for those parts, tanned face and hands and yellow teeth made him look like a member of some secret commando unit freshly extracted from Afghanistan. My companions took some of the free time to do laundry. I didn't join them and as I sat by the fire I realised that I hadn't used soap on anything other than my hands for two weeks. Nor had I changed my clothes. It was getting too cold to spend minutes at a time splashing around with soap and buckets. John claimed at that stage not to have removed his thermal underwear for three weeks. Not once, for any reason.

Opposite:
Oboos (Buryat shrines)
(J.B.)

In that grubby, marshy little camp in Nizhny Angarsk we rested the horses for three days and cooked and cooked and cooked. It was the start of harvest time and we'd been able to buy all sorts of fresh vegetables. We made omelettes and salads and stir-fries, gorging ourselves and sleeping and gorging again. When we weren't cooking, eating or sleeping we were sewing, writing in our journals or fending off the cattle that kept bringing down our tarpaulin like it was the object of some bovine game of capture-the-flag.

Meanwhile Piotr disappeared for a couple of days. He had originally left the camp to attend a service marking the death of a friend of his who had drowned in a storm a year ago. When we finally attacked the crossing to the East Coast, we left Piotr behind for good. By then we'd made a new friend.

1 Czaplicka, M.A. (1914) *Aboriginal Siberia: A Study in Social Anthropology*, Oxford.
2 Ibid.
3 Ibid.
4 Yates, A. (1995) *Siberian BAM Railway Guide: The Second Trans-Siberian Railway*, Hindhead.

chapter nine

THE DEATH OF WHITE LIPS, AND A
STORMY CROSSING

Breakfast was gloomy as we ate our tinned beef before confronting the delta of the so-called Little Angara River. The delta, about twenty-five miles wide, merges with Baikal in a series of channels and sandbars which we shall have to cross. After this obstacle is the dreaded East Coast itself, starting with two hundred miles of steep coastline and high mountains which have awed us from across the lake for the past month.

We've ridden well over a thousand miles. Our good luck thus far can be measured by the basic facts: we are where we need to be, on time, generally healthy and in solid logistical shape. As we fell asleep last night, John and I discussed the luck that has allowed us to get this far.

We'd found the President's cousin at a time when without new horses we would have been stranded on the steppe. The fifth and sixth horses stolen in Mongolia had been taken when we were only two days from the Russian border and our load of supplies and firewood was minimal. The remaining Mongol horses had recovered most of their health and strength and hadn't had far to go. Nikolai had been able to cure John's running eye infection. North of the border, Sarge had somehow not fallen all the way through that bridge on the old Trans-Siberian tracks. No train had come through those tunnels while we were in them. The drought had allowed us to make river crossings on the West Coast which would otherwise have been unthinkable.

If any one of these things, and several others, had gone wrong instead of right, we wouldn't be here now. We'd either be dangerously late into the autumn, with savage storms brewing up and no money to pay for guides and the delivery of fodder, or telling stories in a bar back home. With the weather changing for the worse and the crossing and the brutal East Coast looming, there's a feeling in camp that if our luck runs out we'll be in trouble.

Tension and urgency fill the atmosphere around us. The brief summer of sunshine, long days and calm water is past. The days are shorter, and the winds nervous and fickle, often at odds with the scudding of the clouds above. Berries emerge and wildflowers wither. The summer is good here, being beautiful and comfortable and too short. Winter is the opposite and autumn, its herald, has arrived.

Over more beans and tinned beef around the campfire on the night before starting our attempt upon the Little Angara, we had weighed the two options available to us: ride north past the estuary to the river itself and carry on upstream until we found a bridge or ford; or ride straight across the mouth of the delta, swimming the channels from island to island across the sandbar.

Advising us was a Nizhny Angarsk resident known as Anatole Chagin. Trapper, poacher and petty thief, poet, singer and bush playboy, Chagin was an acquaintance of Piotr's. We had met him at our campfire the previous night. He was impish in stature, wiry and moustachioed like a red-headed sprite of the taiga. He possessed all the crackling energy that one would expect from a man of his appearance. He had brought his guitar to our camp and as we passed a bottle of vodka around in the gusty starless night he sang and played. His singing voice was like the howl of a timberwolf and in the firelight his face went crimson with the heat of it all. He sang about the woods, bear-hunting and women. He'd written most of it himself.

We discussed the crossing. Anatole, who knew the area well from his ranging, doubted the horses would like the Little Angara's three big channels. 'Many channels. Three *ochin bolshoy* [very big]. Maybe horses not swimming.'

'How long would we have to ride upstream to find a crossing?'

'Maybe one week.'

With the weather growing unpredictable and more extreme, money and fodder tight and four hundred miles to ride, an additional week or two now would create dangers down the road. We were cutting it fine as it was.

I looked at Kerim, who shook his head. Taran? 'No.' John? 'No way, man.'

'We're crossing the sandbar. Sergei, please make sure Genia understands that we know this is dangerous and we don't want to rush it.' Genia was in charge of the horses. He was good at everything but river crossings.

'Genia says a storm is coming. Lightning and waves. It will be dangerous on the sandbar. We can't be slow.'

We kicked the fire out, checked the camp was clear for an efficient departure, and settled in for our last night on Baikal's West Coast. The black night and shifty wind felt like rain, so we slept underneath a tarpaulin. We awoke to a grey day and the same tugging, febrile wind in which we had fallen asleep.

In the morning I saddled Sarge early. Anatole was to meet us part-way down the sandbar in a motorboat borrowed from some fishermen in Nizhny. After half an hour's riding north, the small smoothed rocks of the shoreline gave way to sand and duney grass. Gradually the shore curled out to our right towards the East Coast and soon we were on a spit of muddy sand reaching out into the first of the three big channels. Forty yards away across the grey water, the sandbar and dunes resumed.

Two old men from Nizhny and three kids were fishing with spin rods, occasionally reeling in small perch. The wind had abated and the grey sky was bright in a flat, silvery way. This ghostly light, reflected by the lake, and the silence and slow casting of the fishermen gave a surreal feeling to our work as we unsaddled for the swim.

Sarge and I were to go first, after which we hoped it would be easier to make the other horses follow. We would cross bareback and then row the saddles and other gear across in our inflatable dinghy. I expected the ground to be firm and clear on the sandbars and hoped that if we could handle the deep channels we would make it to safety on the East Coast by evening. With almost twenty miles to travel, three longish swims of up to forty yards, and a dozen or so smaller channels, it would be a push.

Several times before we had had trouble swimming the horses. While they were excellent in the taiga they were bad in the water. Sarge was to be lead horse on this crossing and I unsaddled him and took off my shirt, coat and boots. Genia gave me some simple advice and as he did so his voice was uncharacteristically brittle. Some of the deep, distilled fear that I had occasionally felt at cliffs farther south returned.

I mounted up and kicked Sarge into the gradual slope of the shallows, towards the current. I could feel his nerves and I saw his ears go straight back as we went in over his fetlocks, over his knees, up to his belly. As the water deepened I drew my knees up before me and my heels back under my haunches, so that my calves rested on his ribs and my knees and thighs ran along his spine, trying to keep my legs out of the water as much as possible to minimise drag in the usual fashion of a rider swimming a horse. I gripped the reins short and high in my left hand to keep Sarge's head up and with my right hand I goaded him forward with my alder switch, prepared with that hand to hold his short mane should balancing on his back become difficult when, in the deep water, buoyancy gave me less purchase.

We were in deepish water but still in touch with solid ground when Sarge's head and shoulders suddenly dropped below the water. I pulled his head up with the reins and he rose for air, panting as his forelegs bicycled for the ground that had suddenly given way to a deep current below him. I urged him on and he struggled forward off his hind legs. The ground, inevitably, gave way below them, too. His haunches went a couple of feet under, leaving me holding his mane and floating above him while he twisted forcibly to his left, separating us under water.

As he turned he thrashed violently with his hooves, half sideways in the water. I released the reins and his mane and swam out two desperate strokes to escape the kicking that was churning the water white all around me. Sarge disappeared beneath the roiling surface for a dreadful three seconds. A vertical hoof weakly broke the surface and then disappeared. Good Lord, I thought, swimming in the channel six feet away, if he's upside down that *must* be it.

After another few seconds he emerged in shallower water, choking feebly but on his feet. For the first time in the expedition, as he staggered back up the bank and then stood there coughing and shivering, Sarge's

139

often frightening animal energy had left him. It was like seeing Hercules curled up in a chair, whimpering.

The key to our river crossings was that if we got one of the horses across safely the rest of the herd would be much easier. Sarge and the mare were usually chosen as the trailblazers, Sarge because he was the strongest and bravest and because the others had learned to follow him, and the mare because Sarge and the other two stallions would follow her and the geldings would not want to be left behind.

In this case, muscling forward on the back of Sarge's brute vitality had failed. A subtler, more feminine solution was needed. We decided to row the mare across behind our inflatable dinghy and then drive the others into the water after her. Genia would lead the mare by a rope from the stern of the dinghy and Sergei would row so Genia had a rower he could communicate with. Kerim, John and I would urge her forward with shouts and splashes while Taran filmed.

We each picked up a four-foot piece of driftwood and with solid whacks on the haunches from these and then splashing and shouting whenever she began to turn back, we forced her out into the channel and made it clear she would not be welcome back on the West Coast. On the far side Genia coiled her lead rope back around her neck and set her free to graze on the dune grass.

Sarge was standing almost still and with his head bowed, shivering and snuffling occasionally. He would cross last. Tofka was rowed across next and Big Rizhka and Bilugubi, the former because he was reliable and the latter because he was a stallion, were herded in behind him as he was led across to the mare. John, Kerim, and I set up a clamour behind them and Tofka struck out bravely for the far bank. Bilugubi and Rizhka, however, turned back, outflanked our thrashing sticks, and galloped off south down the shore.

We would never succeed in sending any others across while they were roaming free down the coast. So we ran off down the coast to get on the other side of the renegades and herd them back up towards the crossing point. When we had done so they still weren't ready to be caught so we sat and rolled a smoke and when they had calmed down Kerim and I caught them by their neck ropes and tied them to a log near the others.

Fitfully, in combinations of one, two or three, of rowing and herding, we got the horses across. As we rode down the following stretch of sandbar, essentially a fifteen-mile dune with sparse sea-grass and a few stunted trees, the storm we had feared finally materialised. It blew almost due north, driving at us straight and free down the length of Baikal. This wind was the Sarma, the most feared of Baikal's eleven named winds. We tied the horses to trees and thick brush on the lee of

Opposite:
Rowing Karka across one of the channels of the Upper Angara delta
(J.B.)

the island, gave them each a pile of oats and settled in for a long afternoon and night in an abandoned rangers' hut. Every half-hour or so a couple of us would head out to check the horses. They were far apart on the sparsely vegetated sandbar, facing into the wind and rain, too tense to eat their fodder as the six-foot swells pounded the beach ten or twenty yards away.

Opposite:
Storm
(J.B.)

By midnight the storm was easing off. In the morning we set off again down the sand. The second big channel was far broader than the first, promising to require about forty yards of swimming. The deep water started about fifty feet from shore, after a gentle descent to rib depth. Because the spine of sand snaked in obscurity beneath the water's surface and we wanted to make the swim as short as possible, we scouted the channel in the dinghy before attempting to cross it. Before the reconnaissance we gathered six pieces of driftwood, six to eight feet in length, to use in marking the best route. There were no stones to tie to the poles as anchors, so we did our best to jam the wood into the sand. Using the dinghy we started to row the horses across one by one.

Bilugubi, the half-wild blue-black stallion whom we had picked up down on the South Coast, was the fourth to be swum across that second big channel of the Upper Angara. About half-way through the swim, which meant that he was a hundred feet from any land that he could see, to front or back, he kicked his front feet out of the water with a weak splash. Then he went under. He resurfaced and disappeared again. When he came up five seconds later Kerim pulled his head onto the side of the inflatable, where he whimpered his last two breaths and died. Anatole had just arrived in a little borrowed dinghy and, with Kerim and Taran holding Bilugubi's head, he dragged skiff and corpse back to shore. Sergei, meanwhile, was left on a fifteen-foot-long strip of exposed sand holding the three horses who had made it across the channel.

We decided to sell Bilugubi's meat in Nizhny Angarsk. Genia immediately cut the jugular veins to save the meat. We dragged Bilugubi up onto dry sand, gutted him, skinned him and chopped him up at the joints with an axe. We buried the useless parts in the sand, kept the heart and liver to eat, and threw the upper legs and other meat-bearing cuts into Anatole's boat. He sped off to Nizhny's small market while the rest of us resumed our efforts to get the horses across the delta. By now some fishermen had gathered around and we negotiated with them for the use of their barge to help us cross the channel. A bottle of vodka smoothed the talks and a promise of six more meant we had a deal.

Meanwhile Sergei and his three horses were still on their tiny strip of sand, the barge couldn't reach them, and the afternoon had turned cold. The horses would have to be led off their island, across a couple of

Taran and Bilugubi
(J.B.)

Opposite:
Above:
The barge
(K.Y.)

Below:
Fishermen on the barge
(K.Y.)

underwater channels and through a reed swamp on the far side of the channel before we could load them onto the barge. I put on a heavy wool coat and was motored out to replace Sergei and deal with the horses. It was hard to make them follow me into the water and as we went deeper their shying, criss-crossing and turning back necessitated stop after stop to soothe them and untangle their leads. As the water deepened the horses had to swim. Two of them began to outpace me while the third lagged behind. The three ropes were impossible to keep straight and my hands were stiff in the cold water. Three edgy horses and a tangle of ropes milling around me in a tight pack in deep water threatened trouble. I tried to keep the faster swimmers back and they seemed almost on top of me as they pushed past. I let go of the slowest horse and swam ahead, passing the faster horses and straightening their ropes. It was too late for the last horse, now swimming free, to turn back. I caught him when he joined us in shallower water on the far side.

Now the reeds. The water deepened again, though never beyond my arm-pits, and I held the leads close to keep control as, barefoot, I dragged them through the half-submerged thickets. I emerged to a weary cheer from my companions and, after a further struggle to get the horses up onto the barge, half a mug of vodka. When the barge reached its mooring in a four-building settlement on the East Coast, I was shown the fishermen's boss. He was red with anger. I climbed aboard his boat, introduced myself and thanked him for his help.

'Fuck your expeditsy ecologisky. Get off my boat,' he raged.

He was a big man and I took my leave.

145

chapter ten

THE NORTHERN EAST COAST

Opposite:
'Ranger Nik' – our guide
through a preserve
(K.Y.)

AFTER weeks of seeing the East Coast across the water on clear days, awed by the wall of mountains that it presented to our sight from the West Coast, it was exhilarating and intimidating to have reached it at last. In doing so, we had physically and emotionally turned the corner of the expedition. But we all knew that the toughest taiga, steepest shoreline, coldest weather and worst storms lay ahead.

Anatole had proven tough and resourceful during the Northern Crossing and we asked him to stay on for the next leg. He kept the expedition moving with his howling songs about hunting sable and his deep knowledge of the taiga. On skis and on foot he had hunted and trapped through much of the steep, dense bush of the northern East Coast.

One day, deep in the forest, he stopped at the foot of a huge cedar. The tree could easily have been four hundred years old. We had been scrambling the horses up a high, steep hill for a couple of miles and were glad of the break. Dangling from the cedar was what looked like a simple tangle of wires. Anatole explained that it was a sable trap.

'This is my trap. You are the only other people on earth who know it exists. I discovered the sable in this corner of taiga, I blazed the trail. I was last here three years ago and nobody has used the trail since.'

'How many sable are you allowed to take out?'

'Twenty, thirty. In October, a panel of experts declares the personal maximum for the coming season.'

Last year the limit had been thirty. Anatole had taken forty.

'I want to eat,' he said. 'I have a wife, kids. Everybody wants to eat.'

Sable skins, by law, must be sold to the state.

'Recently the state price has been low. I keep the top pelts and sell them, the "leftovers", for $50 or $60. About double what the state pays.'

'Leftovers' is Russian slang for an illegal surplus.

Anatole was in many ways a typical New Siberian. His parents had been sent to Siberia during Stalin's persecution of the kulaks, a class of independent, relatively prosperous peasants 'liquidated' (to use Uncle Joe's word) in the years around 1930. One grandfather and two great-uncles had been executed and his remaining grandfather had taught him to hunt.

At fourteen he had his own gun and was poaching squirrels, hares and fowl. After his military service, he left his coalminer parents in Sverdlovsk to take advantage of the incentives offered to workers willing to brave the loneliness and privations of life in Yakutia, in the Siberian Far East.

'In those days', Anatole explained, 'a good worker could earn a car

there in less than half the time it took to do so in the Urals. Every young man wants a car, and back then nobody had one. If you did, the girls were yours.'

Five years later he had four cars and a wife. In the late 1970s he left Yakutia for the even higher wages being offered to BAM workers. As the driver of a tunnel excavator, a knight of the workers' paradise, he prospered further. These were exciting days for the latter-day Siberian pioneers. They were opening virgin lands, the money was good and the company lively. The bush teemed with bear, musk deer and sable, and the brothels with Buryat girls.

Now he spends four months every winter in the taiga and the rest of the year pursuing various 'unofficial projects'.

He was teaching his fifteen-year-old son the craft of the taiga man: how to build a trap that would lift the sable from the ground so that its thrashing and the carnivores of the forest would not destroy the pelt; that the legs of deer and horses provide the best skins for skis; how to blaze trail marks high enough that the winter snows would not cover them. Thinking of his son, Anatole had written his favourite song, 'Taiga Nasha Mat', five years ago in a winter cabin. The title means 'The Taiga is Our Mother'.

We are readying our guns, warming up the stocks of our rifles. It is not war that calls us but the taiga, and we take with us only those who are strong and skilful.

Refrain: *And again, at dawn, you can hear along the river the sable's scratching sound. We are following the ski trail through the valleys to hunt the sable. Here nobody will hear the cries of our weakness. The dark forest is our father and the taiga is our mother.*

In these hills, our enemies are in trouble. But we have few of them – we know the law of nature will rob the trap at times or a ranger will punish us. If the bullet can't pierce the bear's skull, if the knife slips along the bear's rib and breaks, then fate will scatter the hunter's remains in holes in the taiga and in the dens of bear.

When his strength fails him – even his jaw is numb with the cold – and he falls asleep under a cedar which falls and crushes him, or when he falls through the river ice, nobody will ever find the hunter. Only the blazes of his trail and the hulk of his winter cabin will tell those who follow about his hard fate, about his work which he knew and loved.

About how he stalked the animals in the endless snows, how he worked the taiga with no company and no medicine. Yes, he lived for his children to hear the whistle of his bullets in the howl of the blizzard. And, as he did, they will go early in the morning along the river, following the sable's scratching sound. They will follow his trail to get their sable. And let nobody hear the sound of their weakness. The dark forest is their father, and the taiga is a mother for all of them.

Opposite:
Above:
Anatole – "red headed sprite of the taiga"
(K.Y.)

Below:
Shore or taiga? A typical day on the East Coast
(K.Y.)

The East Coast taiga was as steep and rough as we had feared. Occasionally we found it safer on the rocky shore. If we were lucky enough to have a sandy beach we almost always saw bear prints. For the first four days of the East Coast, we had followed a mother and her cub down the coast, their tracks still needle-sharp in the wet sand. We never saw them but, judging by the freshness of their tracks, they couldn't ever have been more than a few hours ahead of us. One morning, in a small meadow of grass and flowers, we found the carcass of a brown bear. No more than a few days old, it had been so picked at by wolves, sable and birds that Genia and Anatole couldn't say how it had died. On the West Coast we had had to fire a warning shot over the head of a bear when it had come too close and now, as the season turned and the bears started to be bolder as they looked for food to fatten up for the winter, we expected to see more. When John woke up the next morning he held his hands open to the sky, wiggled his feet in the depths of his sleeping bag, and said 'Ten fingers, ten toes, no bear.'

Opposite:
In the taiga
(K.Y.)

A fortnight later we caught three 15-pound landlocked salmon. After weeks of tinned beef, the savage freedom that seemed to glisten through those gunmetal scales made me feel as if the taiga were at last declaring us worthy.

The new season was in our diet. The blueberries, which had at first appeared as a signal of the end of summer back at the northern end of the West Coast, soon became saggy and wrinkled, eventually losing their tartness altogether. As the blueberries puckered, currants took their place in our morning porridge. In contrast to the waxy surface of the blueberries, the currants were shiny, their flesh straining red and black skins to a voluptuous tautness. The leaves of the blackcurrant gave our tea some of that tantalising, velvety taste of Allenbury's pastilles.

Throughout the expedition, whenever we had eaten potatoes, *kartoshki*, they had been left over from the previous autumn's harvest. From the start, the potatoes had been rubbery, and the little green knobs growing on their soft skin were pea-sized by late August. By September we had to be very hungry to eat them. One day a ranger on the East Coast gave us a bucket of the new harvest, taken from the kitchen garden behind the little cabin where he kept a lonely watch for poachers and forest fires. Thus far, tinned beef had been just about the only thing that Genia would eat. But that bucket of firm new potatoes sent him into a frenzy. He heaped wood onto our small fire and grabbed the cooking pot from Kerim. He poured its contents – our clean eating bowls – out onto the taiga floor, harrumphing and muttering to himself as he moved. One bowl was still wedged to the bottom of the pot. He tried to pry it out with a knife, a long string of curses rolling out like

thunder through the still forest. The knife failing, he put the pot upside down upon the ground and pounded the bottom with his ham-hock fist. To no avail. Round cheeks red and eyes ablaze with rage, almost frothing with anticipation, he took the pot in hand and slammed it against the trunk of a pine tree. Bang, bang, bang until finally the little plastic bowl rattled loose. He kicked it spinning out into the bush and took the pot off to Baikal for water. Genia's response to the first fresh kartoshki of the year had made the Beaujolais Nouveau dilettantes of New York seem restrained.

One cold and blustery night we found ourselves in a decrepit hunters' cabin at a place called Yakshakan Bay. Poking around the cabin, Anatole had found a scrap of old newspaper bearing a photograph of Jodie Foster. He, Genia and Sergei passed it around with their characteristic noises: Sergei laconic and dry, Genia grunting and chuckling and muttering 'oobah', Anatole jabbering away in a fast, high pitch.

'I would like to meet this Jodie Foster,' said Sergei. 'Who is she?' 'She's an actress,' said John. 'But she might not be very interested in you. She likes women.' Sergei translated this to the others. Genia thought it a little odd. Anatole, more worldly, gave us a truly alarming wink and said 'Guys: *I* like veemen.' He executed a neat jive move across the room.

Genia asked to borrow Sergei's Russian/English phrasebook and fell into a gurgling near-silence in his corner. Sergei was still looking at the photograph. The rest of us sat around and smoked for a while until Genia looked up at last from his phrasebook. There was a huge grin on his moonlike face. 'A-guys, guys,' he began, and haltingly but triumphantly he explained his intentions towards Miss Foster, which included one particularly Anglo-Saxon verb. It was the first effort he had made in over two months to say much more in English than 'guys', 'okay' and 'gallop'.

That evening Genia, Sergei and Tola proposed 'Tamerlane II: the Dogs'. Next winter, they said, we should all travel the length of the Lena River by dog sled down the ice. The Lena is the fifth longest river in the world. We'd start at the headwaters, only six miles west of a place on Baikal's West Coast called Dead Man's Cape, and finish five hundred miles north of the Arctic Circle, where the great river finally spills into the Laptev Sea, an adjunct of the Arctic Ocean, after winding its way through a couple of thousand miles of taiga and tundra. We'd need at least five months and forty dogs.

My journal entry that night betrays illicit excitement: 'After this expedition we might be able to get the Royal Geographical Society or National Geographic interested. Our present equipment sponsors should get good photos from Mongolia and Baikal, so maybe they'll support us again. I might even be able to get a book advance. I wish they'd never mentioned it! Thank God we haven't any vodka with us.'

Our little team was running smoothly. We were cranking out the miles steadily on the penultimate difficult stretch of a fifteen-hundred-mile ride. The rest of the north-east shore, then a few days' hard work on the Barguzin cliffs, and then the long smooth coast back into Babushkin and, soon enough, real life. Although we missed home and were often pretty sick of each other's company, we were fit and we knew what we were doing. We could not bear the thought of this adventure ending, and fantasies of another one were powerful.

And the Lena, outlandish as it seemed, was doable. Anatole and Genia said it would be less difficult physically than the current effort. My journal says, 'Amazing to think we are in the midst of something almost as long as, and physically more difficult than, dog-sledding the length of one of the world's longest rivers in the thick of a Siberian winter.' And few things could be more flattering than to have these men, who knew us and knew the bush, want to ride with us again under tough conditions. It was a most delicious conversation, dreamy, full of exciting details that could be discussed as if they were but interesting abstractions, silly hopes weighed down by disbelief. Just like the first talk we had had, way back in that Massachusetts garden, about this expedition.

As we fell asleep on a beach of smooth stones, the sun long set over the Pribaikalskiy Range across the water, I listened to Baikal lapping against the shore and the horses munching away at the good long grass around the cabin. Imagine, I thought to myself, the sound of forty sled-dogs eating their salted fish. The jangle of their harnesses. The eerie baying as, in Service's words, 'the huskies, round in a ring, howled out their woes to the homeless snows'. Ah, the dream. But were we not then under Siberian stars, by the world's most mysterious waters, with our horses grazing beside us?

We had several deep rivers to cross on that first, northern stretch of the East Coast. Among them were the Tompa, the Orbikon, and Big River: deep clear streams that tumbled out of the Barguzin Mountains. Having killed Bilugubi and nearly lost Sarge during the Northern Crossing, we crossed them slowly and carefully. Usually all this meant was that, after the inevitable collapse of whichever plan or system we were trying to follow, we got the mare across and prayed that the others would follow. We crossed some tricky stretches of water, all the more difficult at that stage for the white-capped waves blown up by the relentless autumn winds. As in the warmer, calmer days of the West Coast, it was very often the taiga, boulder fields and cliffs that gave us worse trouble than the water. The steepness of most of the terrain and the

thickness of the forest meant that our destination on most days was a small bay, river estuary or shelf of flat land where our contour maps indicated we might find tiny meadows or scraps of grassland. The horses, dog-tired after the Northern Crossing and the first few days of the East Coast, needed grass to supplement their oats and open, flat space in which to lie down for the night. If one of these destinations happened to be one of the places where we had arranged for food and fodder to be left for us by the *Anubis*, the need to get there was particularly urgent.

One day, as we rode towards one of our food caches at the mouth of a river called the Frolikha, we found ourselves in a cul-de-sac. In front lay a boulder field, a monstrous slope of straight-edged, sheer faced rocks the size of automobiles. The boulders were highly anomalous, almost mysterious. We'd never seen any so big and the maps had offered no clues of such unusual geology. We couldn't go up and around to the left because the mountainside was impossibly steep and the boulders ran all the way up. We couldn't go down and around to the right through the water because the boulders descended straight into the depths, meaning that the entire sixty-yard water route would have to be swum. We couldn't go back and skirt inland because it would take two days to do so and we were out of fodder and the horses weren't well. And we couldn't go straight ahead as the best route over the rock field included three hideous holes that the horses would never manage.

Anatole suggested we build bridges over the holes and try our luck with the boulder field. It was a ludicrous notion but each of the other directions – left, right and back – was impossible. So there was no way but forward and we sprang into action. A sweaty four hours of chopping down trees, hauling logs, and jamming splints of wood into deep crevices gave us three rough structures laid across the gaps. We tested them on foot and they stood up. But the horses were three or four times heavier than we were. It was getting late and we'd have to try it.

As we prepared the horses, Genia called a halt. He'd thought of something: a layer of moss and grass on top of the bridges might fool the horses into a degree of confidence. So again the mad rush of work, until, bizarrely, the three disorderly bridges were covered in a camouflage of twigs, bark, moss and grass. We started with Little Rizhka, an even-tempered gelding who would follow where he was led and not lose his head. With loud clattering and some dreadful crunches on the bridges, Genia led him across safely. Next it was me leading Sarge. The nature of the boulders meant lots of lunging and jumping and several times I was forced to scramble up the face of a nearby boulder as Sarge came crashing towards me in his dash across the gaps.

Opposite:
Above:
Kerim
(J.B.)

Below:
John
(K.Y.)

155

Tofka, the next horse, attacked the course with his usual brio. Genia was knocked off a rock and flew ten feet down, arms extended with the impeccable symmetry of an Olympic diver, until he hit the next boulder. Good character and rolls of nerpa fat ensured he was no more than winded. Digger followed Tofka and got himself wedged up to his breast in a crevice. He tried to rise but couldn't do it until John had unsaddled him. After a brief rest he hauled himself out of the hole.

Karka, the gentle, avuncular elder of the herd, was the last to go. Two-thirds of the way across, his hind legs slipped into a hole and he fell in, wedged solidly with his forelegs splayed across the top of the rock. These and his head, neck and breast showed but the rest of him was lodged in the tight gloom down between the boulders. He looked like half a horse. We unsaddled him but that wasn't enough. He was old and whiskered. A thousand miles of rough riding had made him tired. After a couple of struggles that got him nowhere he relaxed back into the hole.

Twenty minutes later Karka was still there, almost vertical with his belly against the brown rock. His whole body rose and fell weakly as he breathed. We considered trying to lift him out with some sort of sling, but we couldn't pass the ropes underneath him. We stood over him and tried to help him with our hands but he was too heavy, wedged too tightly. Karka's calm demeanour made him reliable in the bush but in this context it showed itself more as the deadly resignation of old age.

We sat down and rolled some smokes. Every effort so far had failed. In fact each effort made Karka noticeably weaker. We had tried everything and couldn't afford to wait for him. Night was falling and the rest of the horses badly needed oats and somewhere to rest. We'd have to leave him there. If he did extricate himself before the bears got to him, he might try to catch us up. That was the best we could hope for.

Genia, Anatole, Sergei, the four gringos, we were unanimous on each of these points. But we couldn't leave him there. He was one of us, a tamerlanski. Sod reason. His age and gentleness had earned him more affection than was enjoyed by any of our other horses. He'd made it this far with us and he was going all the way to Babushkin and that was that. We gathered around him again.

Whistling and shouting, slapping and prodding, pulling at his lead and trying desperately to lift his flanks, we encouraged him into one more mighty effort. Then, wheezing, he sank back. There was next to nothing left in him. Then one last try. It seemed hopeless. He managed to fold his left foreleg under his chest. He raised himself six inches, wavered, and with a whimper and a groan somehow struggled onto his two front knees and thence up and out of the hole. A great cheer went up and we gathered round to stroke and congratulate our heroic old friend. Truly, it seemed like a miracle.

That northern stretch of the East Coast was a bad time for the horses. In various combinations, exhaustion, sores and illness seemed to afflict them one by one. Each day brought a different problem. Yesterday so-and-so couldn't be ridden, today the pack-horses can't bear packs, and so on for weeks. As early as the third or fourth day, Digger repeatedly lay down on the trail. The first three times, John was able to rouse him. The fourth time, Digger would not rise. We were on the north bank of a shallow channel of the Tompa River, a mile or two inland where it runs slow and twisty through a marshy floodplain before reaching Baikal.

John dipped his hat in the Tompa, but Digger wouldn't drink. John offered him bread, then sugared bread, but Digger refused. Half an hour later he was still on the boggy taiga floor, on his back with all four legs in the air. He could have been a cartoon horse that had just been shot. Occasionally, in the throes of some particular agony, he groaned or writhed weakly. This went on for an hour. Genia and Anatole were convinced he'd eaten something poisonous or been bitten by a snake. We ran our fingers over his chestnut coat, looking minutely for swelling or blood but not finding any. Genia wanted us to pump Digger up with something from our medicine kit.

'Like what?'

'Anything!'

'But...' John sought an excuse to avoid injecting into his Digger some medicine that we hardly understood for human, much less equine, use.

'We don't know the dosage,' Kerim saved him.

'Okay guys, okay guys.'

After another hour the sight was becoming depressing. Digger seemed to be fading out. His eyes were closed. Genia pulled up Digger's left eyelid and then spoke out again.

'Ah-John, John.'

'Yes, Genia.'

'Ah-give me please your knife.'

John hesitated before handing it over. Sergei explained.

'If he dies without bleeding the meat won't be so good. Genia is waiting before... chik.' He drew his thumb across his throat.

For half an hour we sat around on logs in the dark, cool taiga, watching John watch Digger. The only sounds in the still forest were the Tompa gurgling past, occasional soft whimpers from Digger, and the repetitive rasp of steel on stone as Genia sharpened and resharpened the knife. And then, with no warning, Digger rolled onto his knees and heaved himself up. John offered him another hatful of water and this time he drank. We let him rest awhile. The bread was dry and hard so I dipped some in the stream. John held out the bread and Digger ate. We shared Digger's load out among the other horses and carried on.

The human part of the team was pretty healthy. I had conjunctivitis but it was soon cleared up by John, who'd taken over from Nikolai as team doctor. Sergei had started the expedition with great slabs of muscle and they were pretty much gone by the time we finished that northern section of the East Coast. About a week after the boulder field, John bored the fifth new hole in his belt. Six inches was no small loss from a waistline that had run the Boston Marathon just a week before we departed for Mongolia.

Food was only occasionally a problem. Although there were stretches when we had little or none at all, the re-supply system with the *Anubis* was working well. The increasingly unpredictable weather, and its growing violence when it was bad, necessitated all sorts of complicated plans and contingencies with Captain Shishkin. These arrangements rarely worked perfectly, but by then we knew that that was how life worked with Siberian terrain, Baikal weather and Russian logistics.

The team had by then shared all sorts of tense moments. We had pulled through each time and now had an individual and collective confidence to match our respect for the difficulties of the path. We gringos, meanwhile, had grown up a bit. We were harder, more realistic, and more patient. It was a good time.

One night, at a place called Turtukit Bay, we broke out one of the few bottles of drink that we had with us at that stage. Genia, usually the most private of us all, insisted upon making the first toast. There was no real occasion, so I was surprised. Sergei translated. 'When I first saw you boys in Camp Selenge, I thought that maybe by the end of the expedition Baikal would have made real taiga men of you. It has already done so. Here's to that transformation.' I cannot think of praise I cherish more.

Kerim, like Nik, had been forced by circumstances at home to embark on the expedition knowing he had to leave before we made it back to Babushkin. In late August his time was up. Our last dinner with him was on a sandy beach near a ranger outpost by the hot springs at Arshan Bay. He, John, Taran and I had lived together through four years of university. We had slept under the stars at his olive farm, accessible only by foot or sea, on the Turkish coast. We'd studied under his father at university and spent long snowy weekends at my house in the valley of the Hudson River. We had planned this expedition together for two years and now we had ridden all the way from Babushkin.

In the morning we put Kerim on the *Anubis*.

'Bull', he said when I gave him a goodbye hug, 'it's been a good ride'.

'Go get 'em, amigo.'

He sailed off for Irkutsk and the next time I saw him was a couple of years later when I was giving a speech at the annual dinner of the Explorers Club in New York.

In early September we rode into a village called Davsha. To the south lay thirty miles of fiendishly tough cliffs, which would constitute the next and penultimate leg of the expedition. Along with the Northern Crossing, it promised to be the shortest and most difficult stage of our entire route. The cliffs end at a place called Cheverkui Bay. From there on south to Babushkin we expected to find trails, villages and people.

Overleaf:
The Barguzin Mountains
north of Davsha
(J.B.)

7:35 P.M., 1ST SEPTEMBER, NORTH-EAST COAST OF LAKE BAIKAL

Faintly but surely we are reaching the end of the wilderness. The coast is still wild – the taiga stretches east from us in an impenetrable, unpenetrated blanket up to the Barguzin Mountains and beyond for hundreds of miles. Nonetheless I can feel man approaching. This is more because of what I know than what I see, for time is running out and every step south is a step towards the less wild part of the lake. After weeks of swimming across rivers and around cliffs, of blazing trails, of choosing among winding game trails, of simply following the beach, this afternoon we came upon a path of delectable width and flatness. We passed a very tidy farm and ranger's post and then the path petered out into bush. We had, it seemed, entered the Barguzin Nature Preserve.

Tomorrow, we ride to Davsha. We have a long way until Babushkin, perhaps a month. But after tomorrow the days of travelling with our horses through thick taiga and down mile after mile of rocky beach will be over. We'll tackle the cliffs beyond Davsha on foot and then ride on south, inland and through less wild country, to Babushkin. No longer relying on the ship for caches of food and fodder, we shall no longer depend so much on Baikal and her moods.

Two months of scrambling the horses down to and up from the beach, of praying that the mossy, trackless forest floor below your mount's hooves is not concealing a hole as bad as the last one, are almost behind us.

After the cliffs we shall no longer see moist bear spoor five times a day, black and waxy with little red brousnyka berries as evenly spaced as if they had been put on a fruit cake. The utter faith that any water is drinkable, the assurance that the only man you will see is a ranger, the absence of women of any sort, the dead quiet at all times, the knowledge that fresh bread and butter cannot happen and that if the beans run out there won't be more, the fear of leading a major river crossing, most of these I shall never feel again.

I am probably making it sound as if we are about to be dumped in the middle of Hyde Park. I mustn't, for we have almost three hundred miles to ride and about a month under some cold Siberian stars. We have eight badly weakened horses and I'll be damned if we don't bring each one of them clattering back into Babushkin with us. As Yogi Berra, one of the wisest of base-ball players, first said, 'It ain't over 'til it's over.'

With the Barguzin Mountains on three sides and Baikal on the fourth, set in grass pasture behind a scalloped sand beach, the painted houses of Davsha look across the world's cleanest water and through its cleanest air to see the sun set over the Baikalski range on the far West Coast. Behind and around them are millions of acres of forested wilderness. In the days when all a simple Russian wanted could be got from water, field, taiga and priest, Davsha's residents must have felt themselves blessed. It was here that in 1916 Russia's first nature reserve, the Barguzin Sable Reserve, was established under the personal direction of Nicholas II.

Opposite:
A Baikal Ranger station
(K.Y.)

Back then, from man's point of view, the deer and fowl of the great Russian forest provided protein, its berries and garlic supplied vitamins, its herbs and bark medicine. The taiga also provided wealth, for it was home to the sable. Starting in the fifteenth century, as technology, the gradual crystallisation of nation states, and a growing belief in human potential began to dispel the medieval fog of Western Christendom, Europe's dramatic enrichment began to create a vast new demand for luxury goods. And just as the Renaissance prince or merchant expressed this new vigour by adorning his walls with the paintings of Botticelli, his altarpieces with the work of Dürer, his table with the gold of the Incas, he wore the finest and costliest fur he could find.

It is the fate of *Martes zibellina*, a twenty-inch carnivorous weasel that we know as the sable, to be the natural bearer of this fur. In its full winter prime, the sable's pelt, usually jet black, sometimes dark brown or flecked with white, is the softest, warmest, most durable fine fur in the world. As Kiev, Vladimir and Novgorod followed each other in dominating the lands called Rus during the twelfth, thirteenth and fourteenth centuries, furs had been their prime export. In Kievan Rus, the marten pelt had been the standard medium of exchange.

In 1480, Ivan the Great defeated the Khan of the Golden Horde on the banks of the Oka River, freeing the southern heartland of Rus from the Tartar yoke. Having already conquered his northern Russian rivals in Novgorod, Ivan was in a position to declare himself Csar of all the Russias. This he did and Russia as we know it, an imperial autocracy bridging Europe and Asia and ruled from Moscow, was born. Lacking artisans and merchants, its agriculture enervated by serfdom, Russia fuelled its rise with the wealth of the taiga. As Csarist Russia went on to become truly imperial, furs were the principal commodity that Moscow could trade Westwards in exchange for the goods it could not produce itself. When, in 1595, Ivan the Terrible wanted to contribute to a war against the Turk, he sent 400,000 rubles' worth of Western Siberian furs to the Holy Roman Emperor. During the seventeenth century, according to some estimates, private traders alone were gathering about 350,000 rubles of furs annually at a time when a family of four lucky enough to have forty acres of good farmland was earning less than a ruble a year. Most of Siberia's fur was collected not by these private traders but by agents of the Csar. At Moscow a Sable Treasury was staffed with furriers, cutters and appraisers specialising in the arcane arts of the sable trade. The senior staff included a cadre of 'sworn men' bound by a sacred oath to discharge honestly their patriotic duty.

The Russian conquest of Siberia is usually dated from 1581, when Yermak Timofeeivich and a band of Cossacks, trappers and backwoodsmen were sent across the Ural Mountains in search of new sable grounds. Their chief method of sable extraction was *yasak*, the forced payment of fur tribute by indigenous peoples. As yasak and trapping extinguished one sable population after another, the *promyshlenniki*, followed inevitably by the apparatus of the Russian state, moved ever onward in search of new populations.

This rolling extinction of sable from one territory after another was the direct cause of the Russian discovery and colonisation of Siberia. By 1641, the first promyshlenniki had crossed Baikal. In 1651 they reached the Pacific, two thousand miles to the east. By the early eighteenth century, sable were extinct in all but a few pockets of Siberia, stripped out of a habitat the size of the entire United States. Sable had brought Russians to the mineral wealth of Siberia and sable had generated the capital to tap that wealth. As sable income declined, other revenues replaced it: gold and silver were mined, commerce spread and agricultural productivity improved. Sable nonetheless remained an important contributor to the Csar's coffers and the last populations were hunted down in the few remote pockets where they had survived the so-called 'fur rush' of the late-sixteenth to eighteenth centuries.

By the time of the First World War, the Barguzin Mountains hid one of these last populations. The Barguzin breed was not only among the last but also perhaps the finest of all of Siberia's sable. It was for these reasons that Nicholas II established the Barguzin Sable Reserve in 1916. The Reserve was to provide not only a sanctuary for the safe breeding and ultimate repopulation of sable, but also a centre for scientific research into what remained an important source of revenue for a congenitally stressed Treasury. Now called simply the Barguzin Reserve, its mission has grown into a broad mandate to protect and study natural life within its borders.

With our horses tethered to an old wood fence abutting some grassland in the flat of the Davsha Valley, we met with the Reserve's current Director and one of his assistants. Once again, we were deeply frustrated by the cynicism and inertia of the Russian apparatchiks, most of them pre-perestroika appointees, who control Baikal's fate.

The Director started with a veiled declaration that if we didn't represent somebody with money to dispose of we couldn't be any good to him.

'Anything less than one million dollars would be useless,' he said. 'A big dock is expensive, and without a big dock the big ships will never come. Only then can we build the hotels.'

'Hotels?'

'Davsha is a beautiful place. With tourists we can all be rich.'

I suggested we talk about ideas that were more realistic and more consistent with the Director's mission. He shrugged and did not look up from his desk. On the way to his office, Taran, John and I had been struck by the beauty of the village and its surroundings. Now, greeted once more by apathy and disrespect, we sat in a silent room in a beautiful place that demanded our effort.

I looked at the Director and the silence continued. I turned to Sergei and saw in his eyes the discomfort he often showed in these meetings, when he was embarrassed either by his countrymen or by me and often both. Harried by the stillness of the room, I grabbed at an idea that had been germinating in my mind over the last two weeks and started talking.

'I agree that Davsha and its surroundings are so beautiful that rich foreigners can be found to visit it. What's more, there exists in the West a certain breed of people, generally affluent, who pay to be put to good use in beautiful places. It's called ecotourism.

'The visitors could work with your rangers to make erosion-preventing trails, non-polluting outhouses, safe fireplaces,' I said. 'Then the Reserve could take in guests for treks into the mountains and along Baikal's shore. The money from these guests could support your work. You could buy laboratory equipment, winter clothes, saws for cutting firewalls.'

I pointed out that Davsha's farmers and the rangers' wives would receive income from food and services. Davsha itself was so dramatically beautiful that every summer the Reserve would probably have a new batch of lifelong supporters.

Sergei looked quickly back at me, his broad brow furrowed in surprise, for we had often discussed the pros and cons of ecotourism and I had usually said that any tourism at all would be bad for Baikal. But if the tourists' money would help protect the wildlife and advance a scientific understanding of the local ecology, then perhaps the preservationist argument was largely an aesthetic indulgence. Desperate to make something significant happen in Davsha after so many disappointments elsewhere, I spoke as a pragmatist.

Leaning forward and moving his hands about while he translated, even Sergei, usually phlegmatic about the expedition's environmental work, had become enthusiastic. The Director just stared at his desk and played with his glasses.

'With this infrastructure in place, you could attract foreign scientists and their funding. It would be easy to attract a new group of ecotourists to Davsha each summer, people who would pay to help your scientists and rangers with the work of the Reserve. They would bring their own equipment, outboard motors, microscopes, slides, tagging devices. They would almost certainly leave most of it behind.' I paused to let the Director react. Silent, he shifted his stare from desk to window and put his glasses in his breast pocket.

He didn't like me, he didn't like ideas, and he didn't like preaching foreigners. But if he cared about Baikal, his Reserve, his rangers and their children, he could be expected to put up with fifteen minutes of talk. Our only hope of achieving anything was to offer to shoulder most of the burden.

I said to the Director that we could probably organise the project for him. My idea would pay for itself, it was productive, its scale was manageable, its potential results long-lasting. And Davsha was the ideal place: remote enough not to be overrun, accessible by water, picturesque with its carved Siberian eaves and painted shutters, and surrounded by millions of acres of pristine and scientifically rich wilderness beautiful enough to make Baikal zealots out of all who visited. After months of toiling through the sun and rain, over the rocks, bogs and deadfall, after hours of listening to bureaucrats, scientists and extremists, we had found a practical idea and the perfect setting.

When Sergei and I had finished, the Director half-turned from the window and said goodbye to Anatole, Sergei and Genia. I rose to leave but Taran exhorted me to a final effort.

'We have seen much of Baikal and we love it. Please, please don't ignore our offer. All you have to do is write a short proposal along the lines we have sketched. If you care about Lake Baikal, it's a small chance to take.'

But the Director wanted his million dollars of dock and hotel and patronage and as we stood up he did not come out from behind his desk to shake hands. Nor did he say goodbye.

In Davsha we had found the fifth park or reserve where our advice and commitment and our contacts back home could have made a difference, but as usual something had made it clear that any money and effort spent there would be wasted.

Silenced, we walked down through the meadow to Baikal and the *Anubis* to eat and gather our packs for the long walk ahead. From

Davsha to a big cape called the Holy Nose is almost pure cliff. It was the one stretch of Baikal's twelve-hundred-mile shoreline where we absolutely could not take the horses, so we would leave them in Davsha to be picked up by a fishing barge. Taran, John, Anatole and I would try the cliffs on foot. Judging from the opinions of local rangers, we would need everything to go right if we were to make it through the next thirty miles without excessive drama. Nobody, we had been told in Davsha, had ever tried to traverse the cliffs and steep taiga between it and Cheverkui Bay.

chapter eleven

THE WALK

Opposite:
Along the Barguzin Cliffs
(J.B.)

9:10 P.M., 3RD SEPTEMBER, BETWEEN DAVSHA AND CHEVERKUI BAY, EAST COAST OF LAKE BAIKAL

We estimated this morning that it would take us three days to walk the next sixty kilometres, so we have packed four and a-half days' food. Our progress today, through the thickets and deadfall, up and down the steep slopes and along the cliffs and rocks on the shore, was so slow that it is clear that we shall take longer than we expected to reach new supplies. We are rationing the food carefully. According to our maps, three rivers come through this wall of mountains to the lake in relatively gentle valleys. But these valleys are covered in brutally thick taiga and the rivers are deep.

John had a rough fall into the lake this evening. At fifty pounds each, the packs are heavy and our backs and necks are sore. Our boots are ill-suited to this work and the steep slopes and shifting rocks have eaten through our old calluses. Even at this early stage, the candle by the light of which I am writing seems like an excessive weight in my pack.

This afternoon Anatole and I saw a big brown bear, a Siberian grizzly about six feet tall at the shoulder when he stood upright. The threat of more bears keeps us tense on the trail. Except for the axe, as essential a part of all taiga work as a pair of boots, we are unarmed.

4TH SEPTEMBER, BETWEEN DAVSHA AND CHEVERKUI BAY, EAST COAST OF LAKE BAIKAL

For the first hour-and-a-half this morning we waded up to our knees in sucking, belching swamps. After emerging onto an incongruous stretch of sandy beach we saw a black bear, a nice fat male so lazy and full of berries that we were able to approach within thirty yards before he took fright and burst off up and into the taiga. Had he been brown – Ursus arctos, the Northern Asian grizzly – rather than black, we would have been less curious.

After three more hours of trudging along the beach and scrambling over boulders above the blue water, we reached the Sosnovka River. Thirty yards wide and quick, it looked chest deep at best. Trouble. The river was too fast to ford and swimming it under our packs would be impossible. We took the opportunity to liberate ourselves from the packs and collapsed onto the shingle.

Grateful that they would delay any exertion for a further few minutes, we rolled a round of smokes. John, with the heaviest pack, had been silent. Now he spoke. 'Did anybody else see that old boat a ways back?' Anatole perked up, recognising the word 'boat'. He and John walked a quarter of a mile back down the rocks and found the old wooden shell John had seen. They towed it along the shore to the river's mouth, where Taran and I had fallen asleep against a log. After five minutes of plugging the biggest holes with birch bark and leaves we poled and paddled ourselves across.

Today's wispy clouds bode ill but they brought neither rain nor wind and waves. Nothing about Baikal, not its beauty, power, or mystery, is quite so Olympian as its capriciousness. Now, in the autumn, the lake rages with greater fury and less warning than ever. One thousand miles from the tempering effects of any other sea, Baikal creates its own weather. Sometimes it seems angry, sometimes forgiving. It is always unpredictable. We crawl and climb in constant anxiety about what mood the depths will throw up next.

Earlier this evening, we passed a small clearing twelve feet above the lake. Caution counselled

169

us to stop and make camp, but the trance-like urge forward was too strong. We scraped on south down the coast for another two hours. As darkness fell and we worried that we would have to spend the night on the rocks, we came to a sharp buttress of granite reaching ten feet into the lake. On our side of this impasse was a rocky cove about twenty-five feet long and ten feet wide at its widest — not a very safe place to bivouac for the night. At the end of this thin shelf, where it meets the buttress, the land drops straight and deep into Baikal. Anatole shed his pack and tried to climb around the buttress to see what lay beyond, but it was too dark. So here we are in this tiny cove, huddled under a light, gusty rain, leaning forward to shield our tins of beef and to stare into the small driftwood fire.

5TH AUGUST, BETWEEN DAVSHA AND CHEVERKUI BAY, EAST COAST OF LAKE BAIKAL

When we awoke this morning the wet stones revealed that last night's waves came all the way up the slope of rocks at the top of which we slept. A few inches higher and Baikal would have swamped the camp.

On the cliffs today, like yesterday, we spent hours clinging to tufts of grass and to tree branches, inching forward, fifteen, fifty, one hundred feet above the water. There is a miraculous kind of tree on these cliffs, but we don't know its name. Its roots cling sturdily to the rock and its branches arch out from the wall and then upwards like the arms of drooping candelabras. I have never seen anything like it anywhere. Without these trees and their little shelves of dirt and small plants, we would be stranded somewhere to the north, between here and Davsha.

When we are forced over the cliffs and into the taiga the going is tougher, if less dangerous. The bears make the only paths through this taiga and we follow these little tunnels when we can. The webs of fallen spruce and stone pine and the interlocking arms of adjacent aspens form a maze of jagged walls. When we can't climb over the walls we twist through them or try to crawl underneath. Tufts of fur and glistening wet droppings remind us that we are not the afternoon's only travellers. If a bear comes down the path there will be nowhere to turn. We take turns going first. In this first day and a half we have spent hours with our faces in the mud, flat as snakes, wrenching our fifty-pound packs through the branches.

We shout out in violent frustration several times a day, as if lake and forest are our enemies. On a windy day the waves that force us to jump and swing among foaming rocks do not feel like the lake's fault. But when Baikal heaves mysteriously on a still, blue day, it seems spiteful. The forest feels equally hostile. We have felt this before. It is a sensation that gives an insight into the minds of the men who control Baikal's destiny, for Russia is not so modern, nor its land so easy, that its people have left their original struggles behind. Nature in Russia has long been something to conquer. The Siberians we have known often seem to love the wilderness around them for what they have been able to do in the face of it.

Tonight's wind is stronger than last night's and the water is even more turbulent. It has rained all day but now only a light drizzle is falling. We are camped on a narrow beach. Its round stones, smooth and big as oranges, rise about six feet above the lake, sloping gently out of the water until they level off to form the flat upon which we shall sleep. We have strung up a tarpaulin, tying its corners to boulders and to huge driftwood logs thrown onto the shore by the storms of autumns past. After breakfast tomorrow, we shall each have two-thirds of a tin of beef and half

a handful of rice to fuel another three days of climbing and stumbling south.

Muddy and wet, we are lying in our sleeping bags beneath the tarpaulin. We are lying four abreast, perpendicular to the lake, with our heads towards the water and our feet to the cliff. Baikal is raging now. Waves boom into our beach and then rush back with the roar of a million round stones clattering over each other.

We curl up in our sleeping bags, muttering in our exhaustion that the water will not reach us. But we cringe with the crash of each wave. Baikal is angry. Sheets of shattered water crash onto the tarp. Random gusts extinguish my candle. A log, two feet in diameter, is our bulwark against the lake, stopping most of the spray and the long surges that mount the stony slope.

6TH SEPTEMBER, BETWEEN DAVSHA AND CHEVERKUI BAY, EAST COAST OF LAKE BAIKAL

A log crashed through the tarp and onto Taran's head at about four o'clock last night. The waves had risen and risen until the water was pouring past and around our bulwark as we huddled in our bags, dazed by exhaustion and lulled by hope. It takes a lot to awaken Taran so we took the occasion seriously. Shouting above the raging lake, we scrambled in the dark wind, spray and rain to find socks, rain gear and boots. We stuffed the sleeping bags into our packs, gathered the pot and the axe, and climbed up and over a rampart of rocks and driftwood and down into the tangle of rocks and tent-sized roots behind. John and I found some birch bark and used it to light a small fire as Taran put the packs under the tarp and Anatole dug through the driftwood for some dry wood to burn. I soon fell asleep crumpled against a log with a cold rain slanting down.

When I awoke Anatole was crouching under the root lattice of a huge upended stone pine. He looked like a soaked dwarf under a toadstool. Taran had crawled under the tarp and John was shivering by the fire. Before walking on, we boiled a pot of tea and poured it into our sugar bottle, shaking it to extract the last charge of energy from the container.

After the tea we strapped on our packs and pointed south again. After four hours along the cliffs, we saw ahead of us what appeared to be a headland. The land stopped its gentle vertical curve out into the lake and beyond lay nothing but sky and water. Around that point should be a bay. We hoped so, for in the hollow of every bay is a stream, which might even mean a ranger's camp and a cache of food, or at least a trapper's hut with a roof.

We reached the headland, but around it were more rocks. Hungrily, hoping, we followed the slow curve around. Taran was leading us. When he stopped short with his arms hugging an outcropping, I hastened towards him. I saw as I neared him that his jaw had dropped and he was staring out at something on the other side of the point. I joined him and he pointed down to a level valley, two hundred feet below us and on the far side of a river.

In the valley were four flat green gardens and four squat log buildings. Smoke rose from each of them. A dog rooted around between two of the gardens. We crawled around the corner of jagged rocks and dragged ourselves up onto a shelf hanging above the valley. Even Anatole was silent.

Between us and the valley floor was a treeless, rootless cliff. To get around it would mean a day's backtracking and heading inland.

'We won't make it down that cliff without ropes,' said John.

'We've got to go around,' I agreed. 'There's no way I'm going down that face.'

We talked to Anatole for a minute and then Taran said, 'That's it. I'm going down.' And down he went: slowly over the ledge, clawing into the stones that made one side of a chute, sliding through the dirt and grass in the centre of the chute, and bumping and slipping down, digging in and holding wherever he could until, a hundred and fifty feet later, the wall curved out into the valley floor.

Scared, much slower than Taran, I tightened the waist- and shoulder-straps of my rucksack and went over the ledge. The jagged face gave me purchase until it gave way to the chute. Fifteen feet below was a small bump.

I looked down and was so annoyed to see Taran safe at the bottom, looking up, that I dug my nails into the cliff wall, loosened the grip of my toes, and slid down, keeping my hips, shoulders and face firmly against the wall. As I reached the point where I expected the bump, I dug in my feet. The bump slowed me and I clutched at a clump of grass overhead. Stopped, I inched to my right until I was under the right-hand wall of the chute. After the descents that Taran and I had made, there was little left of the moss, stone and dirt that had slowed our slide.

Now John was above me with much less purchase than we had enjoyed.

'It's a blind slide down until you stop,' I called out to him. 'You've got to trust me. Just stay pressed to the face and slide. Dig in with your hands and keep your whole body on the wall. I'll stop you from here if I can.' I saw him tremble slightly as he gathered his nerve. He slid down, slowed as his feet hit the bump, lunged at a root, and scraped to a stop with his knees on the bump. From forehead to knees, his whole body was pressed to the face as if glued.

John and I made it down the rest of the cliff while Anatole scrambled down another way. We walked a few hundred yards upstream until we found a place to ford the storm-swollen river. Wedging our feet upstream of the rocks around which the fast current swirled at hip height, we crossed the river's three channels. We emerged from the last one to be greeted by the dog we had seen. He followed us along dirt paths through the small vegetable plots to one of the buildings. An old man in tall black rubber boots and a canvas jacket came out of one of the buildings and stopped dead when he saw us. For a few seconds he stared at us and we stared at him.

He turned away, calling the dog to him. Who, he seemed to ask himself, were these men? We were plastered with mud and leaves, and our faces and hands were scratched. Water ran from our packs down our torn trouser legs. We stood there mutely, shifting the weight on our backs. The man stepped back towards the house. Then, together, discordantly, we started talking at him.

'Zdrasvitye.' Hello.

'Dobri outram.' Good day.

The man turned back towards us but said nothing. Anatole spoke again and the man muttered something and pointed off down a path. Anatole said 'Let's go,' and we followed him down the path. As John and Anatole walked past one of the buildings, Taran and I stood on tip-toes and looked inside.

On a table running almost the whole thirty-foot length of the building was laid out such a feast as we had never seen in Russia. We held ourselves up on the window-sill by our elbows and gazed at the cruel array. The long table bore piles of smoked perch and salted omul, bowls of grapes and apples, irregular loaves of fresh bread, dishes of butter, stacks of pink wafers, pyramids of tinned sugared milk and coffee.

When the sight had become too painful, we limped ahead to catch up with John and Anatole. They had entered a narrow rectangular log cabin. Taran and I caught up with them in an ante-room where they were peeling off their torn and muddy clothes. When we had all hung up our gear and moved into the bunkhouse in our underwear to roll a smoke and huddle by the black wood stove, Taran nodded stiffly to John and muttered 'My God, Boit, you'll never believe what Bull and I just saw.' John murmured obscurely and stared at the stove. He was delirious from the warmth. 'Boit, you've got to listen. We've seen their food.'

'Food?'

'They've got a bloody feast in there.'

'What?'

'Food, Boit, food.'

'Food? Where?'

'They've got a whole food building and the table's covered with fruit and fresh bread and omul and coffee.'

'No. No way. Fruit? Fresh bread?'

'Seriously. Bull saw it.'

'Boit, they've got a banquet in there, all laid out on the table. With milk and jam too.'

'You're crazy. You're fantasising. The taiga's got to you. Jam!'

Taran and I were too tired to argue and John was in no state to have a look for himself, so we sat on the floor and smoked and wondered where the hell we were until we fell asleep. The camp was too big to be a ranger station and no private citizens could live in so remote a place. Although there were clothes, unmade beds and old newspapers lying about the room, there were no people around. Anatole had disappeared.

We nodded away by the wood stove like junkies on a metro and were out cold on the floor when Anatole shook us awake.

'Guys', he said, 'lunch'. I looked at my watch. Taran, who had lost his, was looking at me, eyebrows raised.

'2:30,' I said. 'They've eaten it while we were sleeping.'

We pulled our boots over our long-johns, hung our filthy brown jackets over our heads and walked out behind Anatole into the rain. In his exuberant red-headed way he almost always has more energy than Taran, John and I have, but as we went to lunch all four of us shuffled equally numbly though the mud.

Walking under the window of the food building, Taran and I did not dare to look inside. We rounded the corner and walked through the door, on the short side of the low, bare-walled rectangular wooden structure. The small front room was clean and warm. Cheery voices, men's and women's, spoke for us from the main room.

'Guyzz, John, lezz goooo!' Anatole led us into the dining room. The feast had just started. Along the long table, separated by the piles of food Taran and I had seen earlier, sat about twenty-five people, ten of them women. The room fell silent as we walked in.

I looked around at my comrades and saw why. John and Taran were wearing stinking blue thermal underwear, big muddy boots, streaks of mud on their faces, pieces of bark in their hair and nothing else. Their jaws were slack and their eyes sunken and cagey. I said 'For Christ's sake, *guys, shape up,' and then realised I looked no better. We straightened our shoulders and smiled vaguely at the two dozen red-cheeked Russians in their colourful sweaters and insulated vests. I looked back at John with his beard and sunken eyes and thought of Dangerous Dan McGrew's entrance into the Malamute Saloon:*

When out of the night, which was fifty below, and into the din and the glare, There stumbled a miner fresh from the creeks, dog-dirty and loaded for bear. He looked like a man with a foot in the grave and scarcely the strength of a louse...

The new audience brought Anatole back to life. He swaggered up to a large Buryat at the head of the table and leaned over him, talking and laughing and gesticulating like some spry little red-headed salesman just released from the salt-mines. The Buryat at the head of the table laughed with Anatole, cocked his head to listen to something confidential, laughed again and waved magnanimously down to the end of the table. I said we would pay for any food we ate, but Anatole just winked and shook his head in his gypsy way.

As we sat down, John asked him where we were. Anatole said it was a semi-permanent holiday camp for the favoured employees of a chemical-manufacturing collective on the Angara River, about three hundred miles away. How this particular collective, of all the hundreds in Eastern Siberia, ever managed to establish such a camp in protected wilderness on the shore of Lake Baikal, we do not know. Nor do we know how the collective can afford such extravagances as fresh fruit.

After introducing ourselves to the people next to us at the table, we stopped thinking and talking and started eating. The smoked and salted fish, the fresh bread and the little pink wafers and everything else that had shocked us through the window earlier in the afternoon, these were but the beginning. Then came heaps of steaming brown and white buckwheat, bowls of vegetable soup and plates of boiled potatoes, lavishly buttered. We finished our allotments well before our hosts had started theirs seriously and then we waited to see whether they would take seconds. If they didn't, we would nudge them shyly and point at a plate or bowl of something. They laughed and shoved whatever we wanted in our direction.

Anatole was enthralling the four men nearest him with a loud stream of chatter. It did not sound particularly modest. The women were concentrated at the far end of the table, near the burly Buryat at its head, and occasionally they would look pityingly at us over the regiments of glasses, tins and food. The men's looks were less consistent, mostly gruff nods of understanding or disapproving avertings of the eyes. On the whole we were made to feel welcome, and we responded by grunting our thanks whenever our mouths were not full.

Pudding was almost the most exciting of all. Plates of fresh rolls appeared, chewy and covered with granulated sugar and filled with sweet syrup. I had eaten more potatoes than the others and could only manage one roll. John fared better than I did. Taran was the champion.

After five of the sticky sweet rolls he was mumbling that enough was enough. He ate another and said he felt ill. John gently warned him that he was going to hurt himself. After 'One last one', Taran reached for the hot water jug, declaring he couldn't eat another thing. As he waited for the syrupy tinned coffee to dissolve in his glass, he ate another roll. And then another. John admonished him a little more sternly, causing Taran to eat another roll with his coffee. He hid the eleventh roll under his jacket and ate it under his hood as we walked back to the cabin.

Out of the public eye, Anatole's fatigue returned and he fell silent once more. He and John crawled into the only two of the cabin's six bunks that looked like they had not recently been slept in. Taran and I cleared places for ourselves on the floor and lay down. A couple of hours later I was awoken by the shuddering of the floorboards beneath my head and the thumping sound of boots. I opened my eyes to see four men, each of them about thirty years old. We recognised three from lunch. Soaking wet, stamping and swearing with cold, they had just returned from work in the taiga. While one of them, a glowering thickset Buryat, applied himself to the fire, a thin and oddly pretty, blond man took a wet rifle in from the ante-room, broke it down, and cleaned it with rag and oil.

Anatole had left the cabin while we were sleeping and he returned while our hosts were still settling in around the stove and into their bunks. He was wearing a pair of black rubber boots that he had found in the cabin, and when he returned he asked the men whose they were. They belonged to the blond man, who did not mind at all that they had been used by a stranger without permission. All along Baikal's shores, we have seen this code of support among taiga men. Whether it is the winter huts, empty save for spare matches and dried bread, or individual rangers who have given us food and have left their immediate plans aside to guide us or advise us, or the spare boats that we have not felt ashamed about using, the forests and shores of Baikal have taught us that effort, lodging and material goods are rarely begrudged by one man to another in the Siberian wilds.

Nonetheless I was surprised by the way in which we were treated in the cabin this afternoon. There was a sense that it was perfectly natural for us to be there, to have wandered out of the taiga and to be cluttering their little cabin. They offered us their own ready-made cigarettes whenever we rolled our own but they did not coo and flutter about us. It is like being in one of those gloomy realist Westerns when the stranger staggers out of the backcountry and into a small saloon and nobody looks up from his drink. It's not a common occurrence, and the story behind it is clearly unusual, but life on the frontier is so numbing that nobody can be bothered to think or emote.

Watching the men come in from the storm and cold and settle into their cabin, I saw a reflection of how we behave. At first they were a group, continuing the conversation that had held them together in the taiga. Once they had hung up their coats, they drifted into their separate routines. The big Buryat folded his sweater intently and the blond-haired man did the same to his shirt. The big Buryat cleaned the lenses of his binoculars and the blond man oiled his rifle. A small Buryat smoked and a thin dark man with a naval pea-coat threaded a needle to mend his sweater. Each man's ritual was leading him farther into his own warm space.

Then the blond man took from his bunk a half-bottle of vodka and poured a small cup. He addressed it with a single neat motion and looked at the floor for a moment. Then he spoke to one of his companions for the first time in several minutes, handing over the bottle and the mug. Snapping the spell, the vodka brought the men together again. It was the first time we had ever seen a group of Russians drink just one round.

We had decided to spend the night at the camp. After resting the early evening away in a *warm dry stupor, we pulled on our boots and walked back through the mud to the eating building. Supper was salted omul, smoked perch in newspaper, boiled potatoes, fresh tomatoes, and more pastries. Still suffering from lunch, Taran was silent and picked at a perch. John and I ate slowly, in languorous measured bites washed down with real coffee and tinned cream. Our hosts were friendly at the table but didn't fuss over us. When they had finished their coffee, the dozen or so men left the building in small groups while Anatole moved down towards the head of the table to talk to the five women. John, Taran and I stayed down at our end, smoking slowly and staring into our coffee. As we rose to leave, the women asked us to stay in the dining room and chat. After nine hundred miles in the saddle, it was a strange and warm sensation to be addressed by a smiling woman.*

But female smiles and laughter were scarier than the bears we had seen during the last days and we could not even look the women in the eye. John put the flat of one hand to the opposite ear and mumbled something about needing to sleep. Taran and I stared at the floor. Anatole laughed and winked at the women and we all said good night and left.

At eleven o'clock, Maria, the fat and smiling young cook, came into the cabin with Sergei and Vladimir, respectively the oldest and youngest members of the camp. We climbed down from our bunks and drank a glass of pepper vodka and ate a couple of pickled green tomatoes before crawling back into the bliss of our damp sleeping bags.

7:05 P.M., 7TH SEPTEMBER, BETWEEN DAVSHA AND CHEVERKUI BAY, EAST COAST OF LAKE BAIKAL

The silent and magisterial Buryat chief of the encampment came out of his cabin to see us off this morning. Craggy and twinkling at his side was the old man who had visited us in our cabin. John, speaking the best Russian among us foreigners, persuaded the chief to accept twenty dollars to buy a night's worth of vodka and some fresh eggs next time they saw a ship. We stood up straight as we strapped the packs to our backs and then stepped forward one at a time to say thanks and farewell.

Hanging nervously behind the two elders were the last two women we shall see for some time. They came forward together and we each kissed them shyly on one cheek. Three of the younger men were working on an outboard motor under the eave of a nearby cabin and they did not look up as we pulled our hoods over our brows and set off south into the rain, leaving them all in Brigadoon.

I turned back after ten paces and only the young men remained outside. One of them looked up, catching me straight in the eye. I nodded quickly and reverted to staring at John's heels as they led me down the beach. Forty more paces and the old trance came back. Another forty and the blisters turned numb.

We stayed to the shore for the first hundred and fifty yards but Baikal was up, booming and sucking among the boulders. Clinging to a branch on a ledge between two high rocks, I was soaked within two minutes of our departure as I paused to time a jump between the swells. It would be hopeless to continue that way along the base of the cliff, so we headed back up the heights. The taiga was steep and with the cliff below it we were often a hundred yards above the lake but rarely more than a bad fall or a rotten branch from the crashing waves. I don't know how plants grow up there, but grow they do. In places it is almost like a rain forest. Ferns, moss, lichens, mushrooms and the other wet things flourish. Progress through it all was a matter of wedging one's feet against the uphill side of the thin tree trunks and swinging from an overhanging branch of the next tree in a lunge for the nearest foothold forward.

We had tried throughout the cliffside trek to keep to a regime of an hour's struggle and then five minutes' rest, but by now we were stopping every half hour. Soon it was every twenty minutes that we'd hang the packs from a branch and one of us would roll a thin cigarette from the remaining tobacco and around it would go, wet and stained, from one cut and shaking hand to the next.

Opposite:
Boris, captain of
the *Anubis*
(J.B.)

We realised quite soon that Taran was consistently lagging behind. For the last six hundred miles he'd been the strongest about illness, injury and fatigue, so the fourth time that we stopped to wait John asked him if he was alright.

'Fine. Nothing wrong. Just checking my shoe laces.'

'Don't they have double knots in England?' I couldn't help myself.

'Fuck off, Bull. Just keep going.'

We carried on, John leading, until ten minutes later Anatole whistled us to stop. I heard Taran retching from about fifty yards back through the woods. When he caught up two minutes later he admitted that he was ill. About ten times during the next seven hours, perhaps once for every roll from lunch the day before, Taran provided the rest of us with a break while he squatted and vomited a few dozen paces back.

About an hour ago we came to a pebble beach and pitched camp. Taran is in his sleeping bag and so am I. We are all haggard and exhausted and last night's cabin seems as far away as Paris.

When we stopped this evening Taran was ill. John immediately checked his camera and then cut and sharpened four stakes, gathered suitable rocks, and used them to set up the tarp for us to sleep under. Anatole gathered wood, lit a fire and put the kettle on it. I said I had to write and burrowed into my sleeping bag by the fire. I occasionally scribbled or pretended I was thinking of something to write, but really I was just sitting hunched in my sleeping bag.

This happens to me too often. I am supposed to be the leader of this expedition and I worry that I am too small for the task. I shirk duties, am stubborn, counsel the short route when the longer is safer. I pretend to write when I am really watching the others at their own tasks. Part of it is that I am not really the leader at all. It is really a nominal position, entailing little more than that I am the one who communicates our decisions to the Russians, and it is a position that I am in by default, having led the planning. John, Taran and I are friends above all else. We have known each other for too long to want to be the first one up in the morning just to impress the others.

But I still try to do it and when I fail it bothers me.

7:40 P.M., 9TH SEPTEMBER, CHEVERKUI BAY, EAST COAST OF LAKE BAIKAL

It's over. We descended from the taiga to see the Anubis shortly after seven o'clock this evening. With whoops and yells and slaps on the back, we came down through the crumbling, empty buildings of the Cheverkui Bay ranger station to be met with handshakes and congratulations from Boris and his crew. After a few 'after' photographs, we climbed aboard. Taran's first act was to lower a bucket of water off the stern and take a long draught of lake water. Baikal, our nemesis during the stormy nights and days on its cliffs and thin beaches, was our friend again. We

gathered in the warm fore-cabin to share coffee, perch soup and a delicious, dazed exhaustion.

We are now at a loss for something to do. We do not want to, and cannot, do anything productive. But after the cliffs the inactivity is bewildering. With nothing to do but drink tinned coffee and surgared milk and enjoy other things that were too heavy to carry on our backs, I am disoriented.

Boris has told me that the storms had prevented the barge from collecting the horses from Davsha. The Anubis, a shallow hulled river boat, had braved six-foot swells to cross here yesterday morning. We have no rice, no spaghetti, no beef, and only two more tins of coffee. We do not know where we shall find more food. Our diet was pretty boring when all we ate was beef, beans, rice and spaghetti and it will now become either even more boring or much more interesting. Taran has found half a bottle of whisky among his gear in the hold, so we won't start thirsty.

The going today was tough but not our worst: trees giving way under cracked hands and thin clear streams muddied under blistered feet. We went up and down two small mountains, stopping to rest and enjoy the views on the second. We had spent so long with our eyes to the mud and rock that the sensation of open space was exhilarating. The furry folds of taiga stretched away a thousand miles beyond a foreground dappled red and yellow where the birch and alder are turning with the autumn. We stopped for a rest in a grove of yellowed birches and round lichened boulders and it was just like those small outcroppings in Thoreau's Concord woods. The air was cold and the sky so crisp and blue that you could have broken it if you could only have thrown a stone high enough.

At three o'clock this afternoon, after a long look at the map and down the line of cliffs, we decided we were no more than a mile or two from Cheverkui Bay and the supply ship.

'We'll be there by four o'clock,' said John.

'No,' said Taran. 'Longer. The taiga won't let us go so easily.'

We decided that we'd be on the Anubis by five. But the ridges kept coming and right until the last ten minutes we feared that the next visible headland was not Cheverkui. At seven o'clock we found a path.

Could it signify people? The rain had washed away all tracks and the trees were unmarked. A human trail would have been blazed with axe cuts into every tenth tree or so, five feet off the ground so that the trail could be followed over the winter snow. If it was a game trail it would probably avoid our destination — the ranger station at Cheverkui Bay — by a wide margin. Then we saw cow shit. Rarely is such a prosaic sight greeted with such exalted sentiments.

The path went down and down gently, a few wood buildings came in sight, and at last we saw a ship moored at a dock. An instinctive look for the expedition flag confirmed that the ship was the Anubis. Tomorrow, if Baikal allows us to cross to the Holy Nose, we shall see our horses. We'll swing our legs over our saddles and point Sarge, Digger, old Karka and the others south again for the last three hundred miles.

10:00 P.M., 10TH SEPTEMBER, KURBULIK, ON THE HOLY NOSE, EAST COAST OF LAKE BAIKAL
At about eight o'clock last night Taran, John and I were leaning against the railings on the ship's stern in the cold and windy night, finishing the whisky and discussing how we could feel its hot trail all the way down into our stomachs. Nikolai Tolstoy, Boris's mate on the Anubis, emerged

from the fo'c's'le and joined our little huddle. Taran held out the whisky bottle but Nikolai said no, as he always does. Then he winked, reached under his coat and handed me half a litre of Shishkin's private reserve of loathsome and nameless alcohol.

Nikolai – Kolya – is always saving us in quiet ways and we thanked him warmly as he returned below decks. Still aching from the trek, I stuffed the new bottle into my wool coat and we returned our focus to the whisky and the cold night. Overhead in the moonless sky scudding clouds erased swaths of stars. At our feet the oily deck moved gently as Baikal ground the Anubis against her mooring. To left and right the headlands of Cheverkui Bay stretched out dimly in the dark like the curved horns of a Highland bull. We shuddered down the whisky and applied ourselves to Boris' hooch. Beyond the bay lay Baikal, brooding quietly on her next mood.

The intense, immediate focus of the last days faded away as the liquor numbed us. We knew that in about a month's time we would be home. We ached for warmth and food and certitude, for even a smile and an honest kiss goodbye from a pretty girl. But we knew we would have those things at the price of the cold crystalline water and the sound of dying fires and grazing horses as we fall asleep.

I also knew that soon we would yearn for the simple determination of every morning wiping the dew from our horses' backs and throwing on the saddle pad and then the saddle, of filling the saddle bags with tinned beef and rice and tying our sleeping bags on top, then slipping the old re-stitched bridles over our horses' heads, coiling up the extra rope and swinging into the stirrups. And we would miss doing it all together.

As we choked the bottle dry and stared out over the water, Kolya climbed aboard from the shore and entreated us to join him and the others in the banya. We felt too shaky to face the furnace but he was so kind and earnest that we hated to seem churlish. We followed him ashore and up a path, stopping to remove our boots at the door of the square wooden banya. Kolya entered first and as he opened the door the smells of cigarette smoke, steam, alcohol and sweat came billowing out with sickening warmth.

A large square table bearing assorted bottles, candles and tobacco occupied the centre of the room and on benches around it were six glistening and naked Siberian men. The iron stove and the buckets of water were in an adjacent room but heat and damp emanated from every wall of the main chamber. The heat and smell and noise almost overwhelmed us in the candle-lit gloom. Seeing Boris slumped over at the head of the table, I thought that maybe we could escape unscathed. But Anatole shouted out a welcome and the three rangers lifted their label-less bottles in our direction and there was nothing for it but to strip off our clothes and wade in.

We sat down on the benches, introduced ourselves to the rangers, and joined them in a toast to Baikal before stumbling next door. I was close to falling asleep on one of the slatted seats when I was brought round by the sound of John shouting 'Yaaahh, yaaahh, harasho, ochin harasho!' ['Good, very good!'] I looked up to see Taran laughing hysterically and Sasha, the largest of the rangers, thrashing John's back with the traditional faggot of thin, leafy birch branches. I fled before it was my turn.

Taran soon joined me back at the table, where the toasts were still going around. Anatole had brought his guitar from the ship and he howled out his crazy taiga songs and the bottles of one-eighty proof grain alcohol passed from hand to hand. I went outside to piss and catch my

breath. As I punched my arms about in the air to revive myself, Sasha emerged with a centurion's belch. He saw my punching motions and put up his fists with a laugh. I laughed too, until I saw that he wasn't joking. I suggested that it might be time for a drink, but there was no denying him. He got the better of me as we sparred naked in the freezing night.

Anatole was still screaming and pounding his guitar as we staggered back into the room. Sasha filled my glass as we sat down at the table and then grabbed Anatole's guitar and handed it to me. I would much rather be thrashed naked in a cold Siberian night by a drunken ranger than do anything musical in public. I handed the instrument to John, who sang 'Bad, Bad Leroy Brown' until he thought there was a danger of the Russians' recognising that he was just repeating the first two verses, and then Taran and I joined him for three renditions of the refrain to 'Ten Thousand Men of Harvard'. School songs were among the academic experiences for which Taran had been too busy at university, so he shrieked unintelligibly and banged a plastic bottle on the table.

I awoke at seven thirty in the morning, shivering in the cold that had drifted in as the fire died during the night. Finding myself naked and half-blind on a wooden shelf in a bare and filthy room, I despaired. I heard groans from the other side of the room and thought I recognised Taran's voice.

'Taran, is that you?'

'I think so,' he said.

'Where are we?'

'Somewhere in bloody Siberia.'

I opened the banya door and the sunlight almost floored me. Tied to her mooring, the expedition flag cracking smartly in a stiff Baikal breeze, was the Anubis. Later that morning, she took us across Cheverkui Bay to the Holy Nose, where Genia, Sergei and the horses awaited.

Opposite:
Above:
Taran gets a haircut aboard the *Anubis*
(K.Y.)

Below:
Kolya
(J.R.)

chapter twelve

THE HOLY NOSE, WILD HORSES, AND BACK TO BABUSHKIN

Opposite:
Shoeing Malish
(J.B.)

T**HE Holy Nose peninsula would be an island were it not connected to Baikal's East Coast by a marshy sandbar. North of the sandbar, the water between the Holy Nose and the East Coast is called Cheverkui Bay. South of the sandbar is Barguzin Bay. In the crook of this bay, the Barguzin River enters Baikal after a hundred miles of draining the eastern watershed of the Barguzin Mountains.

Genia, Sergei and the horses had been taken by their fishing barge from Davsha across Cheverkui Bay to the village of Kurbulik. Six days of rest, good grass and plentiful oats had transformed our little herd. In Davsha we had left eight ill and battered nags. In Kurbulik we found them sleek and perky, their thick winter coats coming on well and providing a robust, healthy air. After the miserable trek along the Barguzin cliffs, seeing the horses again and finding them fresh and healthy gave us renewed energy. Not until then, until I felt that uncannily physical transfer of spirit, had I realised how firm the bond between horses and men had become.

We walked into the village to see if we could buy any fresh eggs or vegetables. Kurbulik is a picturesque place. A loose row of eight *izbas* – traditional wooden Siberian village houses with their kitchen gardens, mostly harvested now, behind stockades and white picket fences – is separated from Cheverkui Bay by a thirty-yard strip of yellow sand. At one end of the beach is a ramshackle dock, and along the beach is a motley collection of wooden fishing dories and dented old aluminium dinghies. Behind a small headland, more izbas line a little valley poking in towards the interior of the Holy Nose.

Into this idyll set off the intrepid Tamerlane boys with their hangovers and blistered feet. Anatole led the way into various kitchens and intensively cultivated gardens. With the summer over and winter coming on fast, most of the families wanted to keep their vegetables for themselves. In the long months between the first snows in late September and the melting of Baikal's ice in late May, the produce of their gardens and a rough harvest of cranberries from the marshes and wild garlic from the forest floor provided their only supplies of starch and vitamins B and C.

Luckily Anatole was a genius with the ladies. He winked, he ogled, he made them laugh. He worked his magic through the village and after an hour and a half we had a rucksack full of cucumbers, potatoes, eggs, onions and other treasures. It seemed to us that there were an awful lot of children in the village. John mentioned this to a young mother. She was pretty, with fair hair and high, broad cheekbones. The northern

185

lights twinkled from those wide Slavic eyes as she answered him. 'The winters are long. We have no electricity...'

The next morning we saddled up and rode south once more. We had three glorious canters on the flat trails and packed sand of the Holy Nose, rolling along in the cold metallic sunlight of a perfect autumn day. At lunch time the next day we rode onto the Barguzin River ferry along with four pedestrians, two motorcycles, a retired army lorry and a man and his young daughter sitting upon a cart drawn by a fine little black mare.

The ferry was an old timber barge lashed to a squat, pugnacious tugboat that groaned with the muscle of a huge engine. The driver, surprise, surprise, was drunk. He was wild-eyed, bearded and reeling, Captain Ahab clutching the helm in high seas off Cape Horn. Once, twice, three times he came roaring up to the dock, pulled the wheel hard down to starboard and cut the engine. The first time he missed the dock altogether. The second time, barge and tug slammed into the dock with a thunderous crash that sent us all staggering. The third go was a success. After crossing a hundred and fifty yards of water the driver brought us smoothly to rest on the far side of the Barguzin River.

There, in a town called Ust Barguzin, we settled down in the soot and gravel of the dockside wasteland to cook our lunch. Among heaps of rubble and the rusting hulls of old fishing boats we found scraps of driftwood and pointy posts from old stockade fences. A fire soon fought off the chill of an onshore breeze. It was a dreary spot and a dusting of coal particles had soon settled over our food, but for all that there was something picturesque about the place. As the beef and beans cooked in the creosote smoke of our fire, Anatole wandered off like an alleycat into the wreckage.

'Where's he going, Sergei?'

'Looking for something to steal.'

'Food?'

'No, just something useful. Whatever he might find. He is a scavenger.'

Yes, I thought, a born survivor. It occurred to me that Anatole and the New York City cockroach were likely to be the only organisms of any biological complexity to survive the nuclear holocaust. Returning to the fire, he emerged from behind a toppled crane and walked towards us like a premonition of the post-apocalyptic order. As he approached I saw that in each hand he held what looked like a dirty white grapefruit.

'Salt,' he said in Russian. 'For the horses.' Another triumph.

We made camp on the outskirts of town in a huge, marshy meadow stretching towards the taiga and mountains a mile or so inland. Dr Yukhnin had driven up from Irkutsk to re-establish contact with us and he and the truck joined us in the meadow. Driving the truck was our old

Opposite:
Above:
Kurbulik residents before a swim
(J.B.)

Below:
Genia aboard the *Anubis*
(J.B.)

friend Kolya from the *Anubis*. Yukhnin, with his bear's chest and mechanic's handshake, berated us for being puny.

That evening, Yukhnin told us we'd done well on the Barguzin cliffs. 'Strong, Doctor, strong.'

'Yeps, boys. Very strong.' Yeps was how he said yes.

For all his bluster, Yukhnin could be an insightful, sophisticated man. Time and again when things went awry and all seemed chaos, he would say something like, 'Oh, guys, I think maybe not so big problem. In Bible, very strong citation: New day, new problem. Yeps, I think maybe everything okay.' Then, in his robust way, he would make things happen to create a solution. His greatest gift in this regard was an ability to deal with other Russians. Officious bureaucrats, antisocial rangers, recalcitrant shopgirls, drunk Buryats, he could win over all of them. For twenty years he had been organising and leading expeditions in Kazakhstan, the Caucasus, Yakutia and everywhere else where Soviet writ ran and the planet's moving plates made life interesting for seismologists. Nobody could charm and bully like the Doctor.

That day Yukhnin had found a blacksmith in Ust Barguzin and good work had been done during the afternoon. We'd conquered the Barguzin cliffs and enjoyed two days of glorious fast riding on the Holy Nose and its isthmus. Anatole, sadly, would be leaving us in a day or so. The remaining team, now composed of Genia, Sergei, John, Taran and myself, was lean and harmonious. The horses looked and felt better than they had in weeks. The way forward was relatively clear, a final stretch of three hundred miles over trails, fields, steppe and small roads until we rode once more into Babushkin. We were all a little haggard and the horses suffered from a deep fatigue belied by their newly fresh appearance, but all in all God was in his heaven and a successful conclusion was at last within reach.

And a superb supper was on the fire. A great pot of Yukhnin's Worpi Soup, named after the superlative batch made for Nikolai's send-off, bubbled away merrily. A fresh jar of mayonnaise awaited spooning out into our various mugs. When the soup had been ladled out, as the mayo was passed around, Yukhnin opened a bottle of vodka.

'Strong, guys, very strong,' he said, eyes furrowed in a most serious manner. 'You have come long distance, many complicated situations. Now you have just weeks until Babushkin. March-route not very difficult, Genia and Sergei strong companions. I think maybe not so big problems. But concentration is very important, so now small vodka for head.'

'And for stomach, Doc.'

'Yeps, guys, for digestion also.' He whacked John in the solar plexus.

Yukhnin made his way back towards Irkutsk in the morning and the rest of us stayed another day in our huge, muddy meadow as Genia took more horses to the blacksmith. As I washed the dishes after breakfast, a dreary chore which I would at any time have happily traded for a day in the thickest taiga Borhan could devise, a huge wild stallion came thundering across the field. After a brief moment of marauding through our herd, he focused upon the mare.

She was a dreadful horse, bolshy, baulky and nervous, an arm-wrencher of the most awful sort as a pack-horse and a zig-zagger as a mount. In most circumstances the intruder would have been welcome to her, but we knew that if we failed to deliver her back to her owners at the end of our great circle we'd have to pay for her. She was tied to a stake in the grass and the stallion chased her around in circles. Sarge began to snort terribly and paw the ground, straining at his rope until I thought it would break. Sergei and Taran ran shouting out into the field and the stallion disappeared at a gallop across the meadow and into the forest.

After lunch, Sergei asked a man walking past our camp whether he knew anything about the horse.

'He lives free in the taiga,' the man said. 'He has captured three of the village mares to be his harem.'

The stallion returned that evening and refused to be driven away. We had a closer look at him and a magnificent beast he was. We thought he was the most beautiful horse we'd ever seen and the contrast to our own tired herd endowed him with an air of almost supernatural vitality. His coat was luminous with health; he was fast, so that his uncut mane and tail flowed horizontally as he ran; and even from a distance his eyes shone. He was one of those creatures whose natural superiority gives an air of arrogance.

Our mare seemed to like the look of him and Sarge was becoming dangerously riled. The mare was no Constable to look at, nor had she been strictly loyal to Sarge, but an affair with an outsider was unacceptable. We couldn't let the stallion continue unsettling our own horses and we couldn't drive him away, so we decided to immobilise him. We put the mare on a very short tether and laid a large-looped slipknot on the grass behind her, securing the other end to a tree. The stallion kicked and bucked wildly when we'd trapped him. He fell a couple of times and we determined to secure him in a way that made him less likely to hurt himself. With a trail of oats leading to the tree, we brought him closer and closer, shortening the rope all the while until John and Taran roped him around the neck.

For the moment, the world was a safer place. But what to do with the stallion when we rode on in the morning? We wanted to sell him, or

Overleaf:
Taiga horse
(J.B.)

189

take him with us to substitute for Bilugubi at the end of the ride, but we worried that he had an owner. Anatole, predictably, argued that we should keep him.

We asked as many people as we could, including the blacksmith, if the stallion had an owner. Everybody said no, that we had captured him and he was ours. Genia pointed out that if we asked around too much somebody would claim the horse spuriously. All the more reason to stop deliberating and take him with us, said Anatole.

In the morning, we were saddled-up and ready to ride with our prize in tow when a grubby little boy of about eight years appeared near our camp, bridle in hand. He had come out to retrieve one of the domesticated geldings pastured in the meadow. Did he know the stud?

'Of course, he belongs to the Old Man.'

This child, like so many who are older than their years, had the self-possessed air of a born liar. Genia went off with him to talk to his parents. The parents confirmed the story and said that the Old Man had agreed to sell the horse to somebody for 300,000 rubles. Whoever this was would get a whole lot of horse for his $300.

We encountered several other long-maned wild horses living in the taiga as we rode on south. We usually found them in grassy meadows deep in the woods. They were always sleek and luminous and charged with a feral aggression. Each time we saw them it was a shock to think that we were in a place where horses ran free, feeding, reproducing and defending themselves, just like any other wild mammal of the forest.

The taiga horses, invariably aggressive, had to be fought off like pirates. Sarge was liable to become dangerously involved in these missions. Digger and the geldings, on the other hand, lacking Sarge's hormonal volatility, could be deployed more judiciously in riding off the intruders. For a week or so we loaded our pockets and saddle bags with rocks every morning. Our expedition flag features a medieval image of a Mongol horseman firing an arrow directly backwards at a full gallop. We never mastered this particular cavalry skill, but we did make it down the East Coast without losing our mare to the taiga corsairs.

On its broad, meandering shoulders, the Selenge River brings the steppeland of Mongolia and southern Buryatia into the mountainous environs of Lake Baikal. For countless generations before the enforced collectivisation of Stalin's first two Five Year Plans (1928–38), this land had been horse country, pastureland populated by nomads moving their herds with the seasons. Compared with the rest of Baikal's immediate watershed, it still is horse country. We rode past herds of cattle and sheep watched over by tough little boys with round Mongol faces and fierce old men with the sharp, predatory features of Kazakhs.

On the night before we were to cross to the south bank of the mighty Selenge River, we camped next to a huge pasture, maybe two hundred acres in size, enclosed by a few miles of wooden fencing. Two or three hundred head of livestock, mostly cattle, grazed cold and silent on the grass. A couple of teenage boys, Slavic rather than Asiatic of feature, rode out of a gate in the fence and joined our fire. They explained that they tend the herds on horseback after school, paid collectively by scores of local families owning a few head of cattle or sheep apiece.

'How do you keep track of which cattle belong to whom?' We hadn't seen any brands.

'The cows always know the way home,' said one of the boys.

In the morning one of them joined us for the three-hour ride to the Selenge. He was fourteen and his name was Roman. His horse was a big grey gelding and he rode with the ease and assurance of a young Cossack. We had never seen a young man so confident and self-contained. He said he was paid $150 a month to look after the herds in the big paddock – a big wage for a boy in a country where neuroscientists have to drive taxis.

Roman had admired John's Swiss Army knife around the fire at breakfast. On the trail, John asked to see Roman's whip, an ancient, well-oiled braiding of bull-hide around a smooth cedar shaft, with a two-foot lash that the boy cracked like a pistol shot. He was immensely proud of his whip. John asked Taran and me whether it would be a bad thing to offer a trade, knife for whip. The latter was truly a beautiful object, so much a part of a noble place and a noble owner that there was a sense of sacrilege in taking it away. But a Swiss Army knife is a thing of such quality and, in an enduring utilitarian way, beauty, that we thought it was a fair trade. They dealt without haggling and afterwards each of them seemed to take every occasion to admire his new possession.

Back in June, we'd suffered our first river crossing crisis swimming the horses a hundred yards across the Selenge. Now we were to cross Baikal's biggest tributary for the second time, a hundred and fifty miles farther north along its sinuous path from the steppe to the lake. The late autumn rains had filled the river into quietly rising eddies and we crossed on an old ferry barge. With the horses tied to stanchions and railings on the rusting deck, we celebrated with an extravagant picnic bought in a local town. The horses feasted on bread, fresh butter and currant jam, which the men augmented with a couple of bottles of Georgian champagne.

The town of Selenginsk is home to the Selenginsk Pulp and Carton Plant, Baikal's second worst polluter. As a response to the heightened ecological awareness achieved by those who had dared to protest

against the larger Baikalsk pulp mill in the early 1960s, Selenginsk uses what is called a 'closed-cycle' system of water use and waste management. The water is supposed to go around and around in this 'closed cycle', without a drop ever being discharged into the Selenge and thence Baikal. And what becomes of the waste that is filtered out? A couple of workers in the streets of Selenginsk told us that this toxic sludge is burned, resulting in terrible air pollution. What's more, they said, there are secret pipes running from the plant to Baikal, where they spew waste directly into the lake.

This was juicy stuff but its source was hardly credible. When Dr Yukhnin had left us in Ust Barguzin he had promised to speak to the Director of the mill and arrange for us to meet him. When we arrived at the main entrance of the huge, fence-encircled compound, the whole place was eerily quiet. Selenginsk was more modern than Baikalsk and all the more sinister for it. There were four cars in the two-acre car park. I tried the large metal door and it opened smoothly. Just inside, lit well by fluorescent bars on the ceiling, was a row of gates with slots for magnetic cards, like the turnstiles of a modern metro.

Through these in Soviet days had passed thousands of workers, many of whom were probably pretty pleased to be there. To work at Selenginsk had been a privilege: it had technical and strategic prestige, its cold and remote location ensured that the terms were generous, and initially the housing and services in the new town built to service it reflected all of this. But that day the place was all but empty. One woman tended the glassed-in booth by the turnstiles. Sergei explained that we had a meeting with the Director. He was directed to a telephone and told a number to dial. The Director's secretary picked up and explained that the plant was shut, Sergei told us. I asked him to ask why. After a brief further exchange Sergei replaced the receiver and told us that the plant was temporarily closed due to a lack of money to buy fuel. The Director was at home and unreachable. 'Trust me', said Sergei, 'he will not agree to see you now'.

Here was a new notion for us, a silver lining in the ecological cloud of the collapse of the Russian economy. Throughout our ride we had seen evidence that Russia's poverty was bad news for Lake Baikal. Before we even saw the lake, in the initial ride through southern Buryatia, we had seen evidence of illegal cedar logging which would have been much less likely to occur when the state was richer and stronger. In Baikalsk, we had heard of the recent shelving for economic reasons of various plans to move or clean up the pulp mill that is Baikal's worst polluter. In every preserve, reserve, and national park, Directors and rangers had shown that they lacked money for vital equipment and had told us that their

Opposite:
Above:
Lunch
(K.Y.)

Below:
Outside a shop in
Selenginsk
(J.B.)

195

salaries were weeks or months in arrears. And then there were the more general truths that we saw all along the way. The 1992 Ecological Law was a dead letter because there was essentially no civil society to enforce it. Corruption prevailed among bureaucrats, judges, and elected officials. Morale was terrible among the honest souls struggling against all of this. The temporary closure of the Selenginsk pulp mill represented part of the positive side of the new situation: the grinding down of industrial activity and a near-guarantee that anti-ecological initiatives of any significance would not find state funding. On the other hand, a state desperate for cash is not likely to take the long view on such matters. Foreign capital becomes like oxygen but the foreigners have no stake in the future of the land. They don't care about the difference between sustainable and non-sustainable development. Much of the environmentally damaging activity we had seen in Baikal's watershed was being undertaken on behalf of, or directly by, foreign interests such as Taiwanese construction companies and Korean timber combines.

But, compared with the vast undertakings of the Soviet days, the damage wrought by the current small-scale illegal logging, sloppy mining and unlicensed building is of a relatively petty scale. It is hard to imagine that projects such as the BAM, the Angara dam, the Belomor Canal, or the diversion of the Aral Sea tributaries could be undertaken in contemporary Russia. The Marquis de Custine, writing in 1860, called earlier such projects, notably the building of St Petersburg on the marshes of the Neva estuary, 'prodigies of willpower'. Stalin called the tendency 'gigantomania'. Custine saw it as an expression of 'the brutal self-assurance of a confident despotism', with a measure of national insecurity thrown in. The insecurity remains, but the despotism, and the free appropriation of treasure to enact its fantasies, has eased for the moment.

In the streets of Selenginsk our conjectures were soon brought down to gritty reality. We conducted several raucous interviews with pensioners and workers and their wives, most of whom claimed to depend upon the plant for their daily bread. Sergei told one group gathered around us on Leninskaya Street that we wanted to know how people in the town had been affected by the closure of the mill.

'Ask them,' responded one craggy old pensioner with a medal pinned to his breast. He was pointing at us. 'They're Americans – they should know. This whole thing, perestroika, democracy, it's all a CIA plot.' In the thirties, we learned, Stalin had bailed Roosevelt out of the Depression. Now an ungrateful America was taking advantage of Yeltsin's weakness to enslave Russia. The Director of the mill was a Russian with a German name. 'That damn German,' shouted one of the old men in a voice spluttering with ill health. 'He's almost shut the factory. They have turned off our heating but he keeps his full salary. If I had a gun I'd shoot him.'

Riding out of Selenginsk, we saw walking down the road ahead of us a tall, berobed figure. As we rode past him we wondered at his long white beard, the pack slung over his back and the long wooden cross he carried as a staff. Three hours later, after we had set up camp in a road-side field, he hove into view again, still trudging slowly down the cracked tarmac. John and I walked down to the road and asked him in Russian if he wanted to share our fire for the night.

'Yanny Panny Mayo Parusski,' he said, delivering phrasebook Russian for I-don't-speak-Russian in a high-pitched accent straight from Billy Graham country. If I'd closed my eyes and disregarded the vocabulary he could have been a Chevy salesman ordering a cheeseburger.

'My name is George Walter. Pittsburgh, Pennsylvania. Zdrasvitye.' I would have been less surprised had this tall, blue-robed, white-bearded itinerant told me he hailed from the moon.

He had already walked from Spain to Jerusalem and had once spent a couple of years living in a chicken coop in Anchorage, Alaska. In America he had enjoyed brief fame as the man who walked from Pennsylvania to Mexico leading a donkey bearing an A-framed 'Jesus loves you' sign-board.

Currently in the fifth month of a three-year pilgrimage, he was walking from Russia's Pacific coast to Jerusalem, via Central Asia, Afghanistan and Iran, sleeping rough and living on 'what the good Lord provides'. For three days as we continued south towards Babushkin, we shared the road with this white-maned mystic, the only American we had seen since Ulan Bator. 'What', the people of south-west Baikal must have thought, 'can the CIA be up to now? First they elect Yeltsin, then they shut our factories. And now they send Jesus and cowboys to scare the children.'

It was late autumn, harvest time, and as we rode on south towards Babushkin, dog-tired and aching for the end, we passed through a few villages where the potato crop was being taken in. Entire villages of children, babushkas and labourers were out in the brown fields. Small figures, stooped to the ground, inched forward along the furrows. Families and friends rested by their piles of spuds. It was one of the great rituals of Russian life and the atmosphere was a mix of toil and carnival. Communal, rooted in the soil, shuffling to the timeless cyclical beat of the seasons, it was a Russia untouched by the grandiosity of autocrats, by venal commissars and the angry dreams of urban intellectuals.

The harvest is a time of celebration, when human labour and the rich-ness of the earth combine with such felicity that for a brief moment the whole chaotic struggle seems logical and worthwhile. But these same potatoes that would make a feast of fresh plenty tonight would be eaten

almost every day for the next year. The celebration itself was ultimately a reminder of the harsh and dreary life of the celebrants.

In a few days, we would have a bittersweet celebration of our own, equally autumnal in nature. Babushkin was approaching and with it the end of our ride. The adventure would be over. We were longing to reach Babushkin, for four months the driving passion of our lives. To ride back down its dusty main street would mean both triumph and home. At twenty-three years of age, triumph in such an undertaking was a stirring prospect. The first couple of months of planning had seemed like half-joke and half-fantasy. I remembered a dinner back in Boston at which a Professor Gokhberg, Dr Yukhnin's boss at the Russian Academy of Sciences, had told us that we mustn't be disappointed if we failed in our physical objective. It was theoretically possible to succeed, he had said, but very unlikely. At Camp Selenge, Oleg Massalski had told us it couldn't be done and had warned us to scale back our ambitions. A couple of months back on the West Coast, Boris Shishkin – ex-paratrooper, moto-cross champion of the Soviet Union, and captain of the *Anubis* – had raised a toast to our 'hopeless endeavour'. Various rangers and taiga men along the way had voiced the same sentiment.

At several times on the trail I myself had suffered serious doubts about our ultimate success. All along the way we had known that reaching Babushkin would be the happiest moment of our lives. And with our goal nearly in sight, but a hundred miles or so to the south, it seemed at last as if we might achieve what so many had thought impossible. Going home was something else that made Babushkin a potent notion to us. Home meant parents and clean sheets, girls and food and bright lights. These were things we'd thought about for months. But triumph and home meant the end. What would make Babushkin good would make it bad.

If Genia was any judge, we had become good at the life we were leading. Some of what it took was simply physical. Crossing rivers on horseback, starting fires in the rain, ignoring hunger are not great achievements, but none of us had ever been as good at anything as we had become at these aspects of life in the Siberian bush. Deeper aspects of the taiga man were more important: accepting your weaknesses; knowing when you are relied upon; handling your emotions, inevitably raw after months of fatigue and loneliness; having the discipline to trust the judgement of people you respect. These were all things that we did far better than when we had started.

About a week from the end, Malish lost a shoe and needed to be reshod. Using the technique we had first developed at Boguldeika on the West Coast and since perfected, we tied together the fore and hind legs that were not to be worked upon, spun him around in circles using his

Opposite:
A meal with pilgrim George Walter
(J.B.)

head rope, and leaped upon him when he stumbled. We sat on his neck, haunches and side while Genia hammered in the nine two-inch nails and bent and clipped the lengths protruding from Malish's hoof.

On that morning we had not yet outdistanced Father Walter, who spied our fire from over a hill and left his path to join us for breakfast as he knew he was always welcome to do. He appeared over a small hummock just in time to see us tackling Malish. At breakfast fifteen minutes later I was at great pains to explain to this gentle man of God exactly why we had been assaulting one of our horses.

Around noon the following day, we passed Father Walter on the road south once more. The route was clear and flat and we knew he'd never catch us up the next morning, however early he started. We dismounted on the two-lane tarmac and said goodbye. He gave John two miniature audio tapes of his thoughts on the trail and an address in Alaska to which they were to be mailed. Then he gave us each a boiled sweet and his blessing.

'Good luck, boys. May the Lord be with you.'

The occupants of the lumber truck and Lada that drove south past us as we bid each other adieu must have thought Halloween had come early that year.

We rode on south through grey cold and frosty nights. The fields had been harvested and most of the leaves were gone from the birch and other deciduous trees. The scene around us was brown and desolate and the first snows were expected any day. We'd driven in one of Malish's nails badly, and he started to limp a couple of days from the end. The other horses were tired and we were a slow and mangy little crew as we limped on south.

At lunch on our last day, John cut a pair of maple saplings and stripped them of their bark to make flag poles. He had last done so under a far warmer sun back in June, on the morning when we had first ridden into Babushkin and first seen Lake Baikal. After that last lunch of tinned beef and beans, we mounted up with the expedition and Explorers Club flags listless in the cold doldrums of a flat early winter day. The sun was a couple of hours from setting when we finally passed a sign announcing 'Babushkin'.

The sign perked us up, though the town was nowhere in sight. A broad cheer went around. We took turns riding first, carrying the flags, dragging the pack-horses. When finally we saw the outskirts of Babushkin we spurred our horses into a trot for the last mile of fifteen hundred.

The horses felt our excitement. The pace quickened and quickened and we were soon clattering down the tarmac at a canter. The road

Opposite:
Horseshoe and nails
(J.B.)

bypassed Babushkin itself and we turned right down a path following Baikal's shore. The path rose and dipped, twisted among small copses of birch and islands of bushy undergrowth and then opened up into a small series of meadows twenty feet above the lake. After another hundred yards we saw the place where we had first made camp on Baikal's shore.

There was nothing left in the horses and we slowed to a painful walk. We saw our old campfire and noticed that the tree under which we had once eaten had fallen into the lake, a victim of erosion. At the campfire I leapt from Sarge and kissed the ground. We had done it. The Primorskiy Mountains of the southern West Coast were dimly visible across Baikal. To north and south the furry taiga coastline disappeared into a grey horizon of sky and water. The world's greatest lake had never looked so huge.

Opposite:
Taran
(J.B.)

As we set up the camp, the old villain Piotr arrived with a driver and a big cattle lorry for the horses, which were to be returned to their owners a day's drive south towards Naushki. He looked monstrously seedy in a long, grey leather overcoat and orange track-suit trousers. Taran and I ignored him. Sarge was the last of the horses to be loaded onto the lorry. Showing his usual spirit, he refused for five minutes to be coaxed on board. And then there they were, our little herd of eight brave horses loaded up like refugees. It really was over.

We climbed onto the lorry and said goodbye to each of them in turn. A hug around the neck, a stroke of the curved jawbone, a last word in a velvety ear and then so-long. We returned to the horse lorry with bread and jam, each of us trying subtly to give his own mount a little extra. We returned to the lorry once more when we heard the engine rev up and we said goodbye to the horses for a third time.

When we awoke at seven thirty to a wet morning, Taran was sleeping under Kolya's lorry and the camp was decorated with five empty bottles of champagne, one of wine and three of vodka. Genia opened a secret bottle of champagne for breakfast and we were in Irkutsk by supper.

chapter thirteen

IRKUTSK AND OUT

As the snow fell in Irkutsk we booked ourselves a cabin on the
Moscow train and organised a big dinner. The venue was a snug
log dacha belonging to 'Admiral' Boris Shishkin of the *Anubis*.
Dish upon dish of fresh beef, pork, omul and perch, bowls of soups and
sauces and steaming piles of dumplings and vegetables presented a cor-
nucopia of tastes and colour, as fat snowflakes slanted down outside the
windows. There were twenty of us, with wives and children, gorging
ourselves and singing, and passing the Georgian champagne, Moldovan
red and Russian vodka.

Opposite:
Bolshevik prisoners on the
Trans-Siberian in 1919

By the time Sergei refused to translate any more toasts nobody was
listening anyway. When John delivered a thunderous rendition of
Tennyson's 'Ulysses' in a broad Scottish accent, the Russians understood it at least as well as I did. Shishkin, our host, had long hated Dr
Yukhnin and some time after dinner announced that the Doc was a
'Muscovite asshole' and made a bleary lunge at him. Twenty avid years
of boozing had seen to it that Shishkin was not the paratrooper he once
was. The fifty-year-old Yukhnin was strong and alert as a young buck
and there is no doubt the scientist would have thrashed the soldier. I
followed them outside with a few of the others and we got the combat-
ants involved in a communal snowball fight that allowed them to return
to the warmth of the dacha with face intact.

Most of our Russian friends came to Irkutsk's neoclassical red and
white stucco railway station to see us off. It felt rather more like adieu
than au revoir but we all tried to pretend this wasn't so. Two of the
expedition's godfathers were there, men of substance. Each of them
allowed a glint of a tear to reveal his pride in what we'd all done. One
was Professor Bukharov, the famous geophysicist and volcano hunter
and the best-loved man along Baikal's shores. The other was Oleg
Massalski, chief of a network of twenty seismic stations throughout
Eastern Siberia, disposer of one of the most important transportation
and communications infrastructures in the wilds around Baikal.

Massalski hurt his back helping us heave our saddles and bags onto
the train. I apologised and he said 'It's God's fault, not yours. Let him
apologise.' This was the first religious sentiment I had ever heard
expressed by a Russian. I was relieved that seventy years of secular
utopia had not entirely erased spirituality from the lands of the Third
Rome. Massalski opened a bottle of vodka and we passed it around on
the platform, the Russians looking clean and respectable in their big-city
clothes, the Americans stinking and ragged holding their tents and
saddles. As my long pull from the bottle took effect it occurred to me

that maybe Borhan was the god to whom Massalski had referred.

Genia was there, the huge-hearted, reliable ox of a man, a fur-trapper from a village two hundred miles away, a genius with horses except in the water. He and Sergei had been the only Russians to be with us at the start down in the Buryat steppe and at the final ride into Babushkin, although they had missed the Barguzin cliffs. 'Guys,' he said, trying to find his customary roar as he hugged us each in turn. 'A-guys, a-one more time, guys!'

'Okay, Genia, okay!'

'Okay, guys, okay!' This exchange of okays had kept us steady during some tough moments on the trail. We couldn't ride around Baikal again as Genia proposed, but we hugged him a second time, passed the bottle round, thanked the big boys once more, shook hands with Sergei and piled onto the train, feeling for the last true time that doomed, romantic Russian combination of strength and sentimentality.

The Trans-Siberian was a story of its own, full of drunks and claustrophobia, a timeless miasma of pickles and vodka as we followed the sun west. For the last few days we'd been hearing escalating reports of trouble in Moscow. There was tension between Yeltsin and the Communist deputies who dominated the parliament. In Irkutsk, the Regional Soviet had gathered for closed-session talks. Now the rumours of coups and Siberian secession flew up and down the corridors. All the while, for one hundred hours, the snowy fields and dark taiga and factories and stands of birch trees rattled by outside the windows.

BIBLIOGRAPHY

ALIOSHIN, D. (1940) *Asian Odyssey*, New York.

ARAMILEV, I. (1961) *Beyond the Ural Mountains: The Adventures of a Siberian Hunter*, Chicago.

ATKINSON, T.W. (1858) *Oriental and Western Siberia*, London.

ATKINSON, T.W. (1860) *Travels in the Region of the Upper and Lower Amoor and the Russian Acquisitions on the Confines of India and China*, New York.

AVVAKUM, ARCHPRIEST (1960) *The Life of Archpriest Avvakum by Himself*, trans. V. Nabokov, New York.

BATES, L. JR (1910) *The Russian Road to China*, Boston.

BEAZLEY, R. (1903) *The Texts and Versions of John de Plano Carpini and William Rubruquis*, London.

BESBORODOV, S. (1933) *The Bolsheviks Discover Siberia*, Leningrad.

BOBRICK, B. (1992) *East of the Sun: The Conquest and Settlement of Siberia*, London.

BURNEY, J.A. (1819) *A Chronological History of the North-eastern Voyages of Discovery and of the Early Navigations of the Russians*, London.

BURR, M. (1931) *In Bolshevik Siberia: The Land of Ice and Exile*, London.

CHEKHOV, A. (1967) *The Island: A Journey to Sakhalin*, trans. L. and M. Terpak, New York.

CLARK, THE REV. F.E. (1901) *A New Way Around an Old World*, New York and London.

CLEAVES, F.W. (trans. and ed.) (1982) *The Secret History of the Mongols*, Cambridge, Massachusetts.

COCHRANE, CAPTAIN J.D. (1824) *Narrative of a Pedestrian Journey Through Russia and Siberian Tartary, from the Frontiers of China to the Frozen Sea and Kamchatka*, Philadelphia.

COLLINS, P.M. (1962) *Siberian Journey: Down the Amur to the Pacific, 1856–1857*, Madison.

CONQUEST, R. (1986) *The Harvest of Sorrow: Soviet Collectivization and the Terror-Famine*, New York.

COXE, W. (1804) *Account of the Russian Discoveries between Asia and America; to which are added, The Conquest of Siberia and the History of the Transactions and Commerce between Russia and China*, London.

CURTIN, J. (1908) *The Mongols: A History*, Boston.

CUSTINE, MARQUIS DE (1991) *Letters from Russia*, trans. R. Buss, London.

CZAPLICKA, M.A. (1914) *Aboriginal Siberia: A Study in Social Anthropology*, Oxford.

DMITRIEV-MAMONOV AND A.F. ZDZIARSKI (ed.) (1900) *Guide to the Great Siberian Railway*, St Petersburg.

FESHBACH, M. AND FRIENDLY, F. JR (1992) *Ecocide in the USSR: Health and Nature Under Siege*, New York.

FISHER, R.H. (1943) *The Russian Fur Trade, 1550–1700*, Berkeley and Los Angeles.

FORSYTH, J. (1992) *A History of the Peoples of Siberia: Russia's North Asian Colony*, Cambridge.

FRIES, H.J. (1974) *A Siberian Journey 1774–1776*, trans. W. Kirchner, London.

GMELIN, J.G. (1767) *Voyage en Sibérie*, Paris.

HANSTEEN, C. (1857) *Voyage en Sibérie*, Paris.

IDES, HIS EXCELLENCY E.Y. (1706) *Three Years' Travel from Muscovy Over Land to China*, London.

JEFFERSON, R.L. (1897) *Roughing it in Siberia*, London.

KENNAN, G. (1891) *Siberia and the Exile System*, 2 vols, New York.

KENNAN, G. (1910) *Tent Life in Siberia*, New York.

KERNER, R.J. (1942) *The Urge to the Sea*, Berkeley and Los Angeles.

LAWRENCE, SIR J. (1993) *A History of Russia* (seventh revised edn), New York.

LENGYEL, E. (1943) *Siberia*, New York.

LINCOLN, W.B. (1994) *The Conquest of a Continent: Siberia and the Russians*, New York.

MARSHALL, R. (1993) *Storm from the East: From Genghis Khan to Kubilai Khan*, London.

MATTHIESSEN, P. (1992) *Baikal: Sacred Sea of Siberia*, San Francisco.

MAZOUR, A.G. (1937) *The First Russian Revolution, 1825: The Decembrist Movement*, Stanford.

MAZOUR, A.G. (1975) *Women in Exile: Wives of the Decembrists*, Tallahassee.

MᶜCULLAGH, F. (1922) *A Prisoner of the Reds: The Story of a British Officer Captured in Siberia*, New York.

MORGAN, D. (1986) *The Mongols*, Oxford.

NANSEN, F. (1914) *Through Siberia: the Land of the Future*, London.

NEWBY, E. (1978) *The Big Red Train Ride*, New York.

PESKOV, V. (1994) *Lost in the Taiga: One Russian Family's Fifty-Year Struggle for Survival and Religious Freedom in the Siberian Wilderness*, New York.

PHILLIPS, G.D.R (1934) *Dawn in Siberia: The Mongols of Lake Baikal*, London.

POLO, M. (1818) *The Travels of Marco Polo*, trans. W. Marsden, London.

RASPUTIN, V. (1989) *Siberia on Fire*, De Kalb, Illinois.

RAWICZ, S. (1956) *The Long Walk*, London.

RIORDAN, J. (1989) *The Sun Maiden and the Crescent Moon: Siberian Folk Tales*, Edinburgh.

SANDERS, A.J.K. (1996) *Historical Dictionary of Mongolia*, Lanham, Maryland.

SEMYONOV, Y. (1944) *The Conquest of Siberia*, London.

SERGEYEV, M. (1989) *The Wonders and Problems of Lake Baikal*, Moscow.

SHOEMAKER, M.M. (1904) *The Great Siberian Railway: From St Petersburg to Pekin*, New York and London.

STRASSER, R. (1940) *The Mongolian Horde*, New York.

SUTHERLAND, C. (1984) *The Princess of Siberia: The Story of Maria Volkonsky and the Decembrist Exiles*, New York.

TUPPER, H. (1965) *To the Great Ocean: Siberia and the Trans-Siberian Railway*, Boston.

VERNADSKY, G. (1953) *The Mongols and Russia*, New Haven.

WOOD, A. (ed.) (1991) *The History of Siberia: From Russian Conquest to Revolution*, London.

YATES, A. (1995) *Siberian BAM Railway Guide: The Second Trans-Siberian Railway*, Hindhead.

INDEX

SWEDEN

FINLAND

LATVIA

ESTONIA

...USSIA
(part)

BELARUS

St Petersburg

Kiev

UKRAINE

MOSCOW

Nizhny
Novgorod

Franz Josef Land

Novaya Zemlya

R U S S...

Volga

Volgograd

Black Sea

Caspian Sea

KAZAKHSTAN

Ob

Irysh

Yenisey

Omsk

Krasnoyarsk

Novosibirsk

UZBEKISTAN

TURKMENISTAN

TAJIKISTAN

KYRGYZSTAN